PREPARING FOR
CHRIST'S RETURN

PREPARING FOR
CHRIST'S RETURN

CHARLES
STANLEY

OLIVER
NELSON™

THOMAS NELSON PUBLISHERS
Nashville

ISBN 0-7852-7291-7

Printed in the United States of America
1 2 3 4 5 6 QPV 04 03 02 01 00 99

CONTENTS

CHRIST IS COMING AGAIN!

If you have accepted Jesus Christ as your Savior, I have great news for you today: Jesus is coming again to this earth.

If you have not accepted Jesus Christ as your Savior, I have very sobering news for you: Jesus is coming again to this earth.

For the Christian, the return of Jesus to this earth is great and glorious news. It marks the fulfillment of our life and purpose on this earth. It signals the most joyous moment of our existence—the moment we see Jesus face-to-face and are restored to our loved ones who have died in Christ. His return will be the most exciting, exhilarating experience of our lives.

For those who do not believe in Jesus, the return of the Lord will be a terrible and fearful event. The "Day of the Lord" is described in horrific and catastrophic terms in the Scriptures. Christ's return is not a day of joy for those who have not accepted Him as their Savior and Lord.

Living in Eager Anticipation

The early church lived in eager anticipation of Christ's return. These earlier believers included those who had been close followers of Jesus or who had seen and heard Jesus. They knew how wonderful it was to be with Jesus and they were eager to be in His immediate presence again. Others in the early church were believers who had contact with those who had been Christ's disciples or followers. They had heard the apostles and others speak of being with Jesus and they could hardly wait for their turn to be in His presence. The enthusiasm in the early church about Christ's return was great—His return frequently was the topic of their conversations.

But what about today? Are we to be any less eager and enthusiastic about Christ's return? No, indeed—we are to be just as eager and enthusiastic! With every day that passes, we are one day closer to Christ's return. In fact, He may come today!

The subject of Christ's return often brings about two responses in those who believe:

One, there are those who doubt that He is coming. They take the approach: "It's been so many years, perhaps we have the wrong understanding. Perhaps He isn't coming after all. Perhaps we have misinterpreted what Jesus said or what the Bible means on this subject."

To those who take this approach I have this word: Christ *is* coming again. The Bible means what it says; it is very clear on the matter. Furthermore, God is always faithful to His Word. What He says He will do, He does. You can count on Christ's return with just as much assurance as you can count on all of God's other promises being true.

Two, there are those who fear Christ's return. They wonder if they are prepared for His return. They are concerned that Christ's return may impact them in a negative way. Let me assure you today, if you have accepted Christ Jesus as your Savior and are seeking daily to follow and serve Him as your Lord, you have nothing to fear. This will be the most wonderful moment of your life.

Still others are fearful on behalf of their loved ones, and especially those who do not yet know Jesus as Savior. They have reason to be concerned. Now, more than ever, is the time for us to share very directly and openly with those we love how important it is that they believe in Jesus and accept His death on the cross as the atoning sacrifice for their sins, receive God's forgiveness, and seek to live in obedience and close relationship with the Lord. Today is the day for salvation (see Heb. 3:12–15).

The Benefits to Those Who Look for His Coming

An eager anticipation of the Lord's return produces four tremendous qualities in us as believers:

1. *An urgency for souls.* A keen awareness of the coming of the Lord creates in us a desire to do all that we can now to reach lost souls with the message of salvation.

2. *A priority on eternal reward.* When we are eagerly anticipating of the Lord's return, we are much more focused on doing things that truly count for eternity. We simply do not have the time to waste on those things that are frivolous or temporal. Our focus is on complete obedience to what the Lord is calling us to do today.

3. *A purity of heart.* The return of Christ calls us to examine our hearts and to repent of those things that we know are displeasing to the Lord.

4. *An exceedingly great joy and hope.* The return of Christ brings hope to the heart—it brings a song of joy to the soul. To be with Christ means that we will experience no more sorrow, sickness, pain, or loneliness. It means that we will enter into everlasting perfection and experience beauty, holiness, and wholeness beyond our imagination.

"But what if Christ doesn't come in my lifetime?" you may ask. The truth is, if you are living in eager anticipation of the Lord's return, the benefits of expecting Him are the same. If you live an entire lifetime with an urgency to see lost souls saved, a focus on those things that are of eternal benefit, a purity of heart, and great joy and hope—what a life that is! It is a life of genuine purpose, satisfaction, and meaning. And, it is a life that will bring great reward in eternity. Can there be any better way to live?

Preparing for His Coming

This is not a Bible study book that deals with precisely when the Lord is coming. Rather, it is a book to help us live in a constant state of readiness for His appearing. It is a book to help us prepare for His return, and to help us prepare others for His coming.

This study book deals with only those things about which we can be certain—it focuses on Bible truth, not man's interpretation of end-time events.

The Lord desires for His people to be ready for His coming and to live "looking" for His soon return. Are you among those who are *ready?*

- *Do you feel prepared for the return of Christ?*

  _____

  _____

- *What is your initial understanding about how we are to prepare for Christ's return?*

  _____

  _____

LESSON 1

PREPARING FOR HIS RETURN

So many books have been written in the last thirty years about the coming of the Lord that much confusion exists today, both in the church and outside the church. Much of what has been written relates to timetables of events—some authors predicting when the Lord will return, some attempting to explain certain world events in the light of Bible prophecy, and some arguing against the physical return of the Lord Jesus Christ.

This study guide will focus on what the Bible says about several key events, about God's overall plan for mankind, and about what God desires from us in the way of preparation for His return.

The Bible must be our foremost communication on this topic. It is the reference to which we must return continually if we are to have a sound understanding about what lies ahead for the church and for the world at large.

As you do this study, I encourage you to approach the Scriptures with an open mind and heart, as much as possible setting aside what you may have read and heard about the end times. Take a fresh look at what the Bible says on this topic and about how we are to prepare for Christ's coming.

As you do this study, keep your Bible at your side. As you study each passage noted in this booklet, make notes in the margins of your Bible. Read the passage from Scripture for yourself. It is far more important that you write your insights into your Bible than to write them in this book, although places are provided for you to make notes.

Keys to This Study

You will be asked at various points in this book to respond to the material presented by answering one or more of these questions:

- What new insights have you gained?
- Have you had experiences that relate to what the Bible says on this topic?
- How do you feel about what you are reading in the Scriptures?
- In what ways are you feeling challenged to change your thinking or to take actions?

Insights

A spiritual insight occurs when you read a passage from the Bible and the meaning of the passage suddenly seems crystal clear to you. Insights result in new or clearer understanding of the truth of God's Word. It is as if God suddenly draws back the curtain to reveal to you a new level or depth of meaning. You truly know what you know!

Insights happen to all who read the Word, even to those who may have read and studied a particular passage for many years. I encourage you to ask God to make you aware of new insights every time you read your Bible. I believe the Lord delights in answering such a prayer.

Insights are usually very personal, and they nearly always relate to your experiences in life, either current or past. Insights are related to how you might apply God's Word in a way that is always timely, yet at the same time eternal.

I encourage you to make notes about your insights. You'll find three great advantages in this: First, you will be able to review your insights later in the light of still other Scriptures that you study. In that way, you can develop a comprehensive understanding on a particular study, learning "precept upon precept, line upon line" (Isa. 28:10). Second, you will have your thinking clarified should an opportunity arise for you to share or discuss your insights with others. Those who write down their insights usually find that their ideas and attitudes become more solidified. And third, you will tend to experience even more insights if you are intentionally looking and listening for them. As Jesus taught, when we seek, we find (see Matt. 7:7).

Periodically in this study, you will be asked to note what a specific passage of the Bible says to you. This is your opportunity to record insights.

Experiences

Everything you read in God's Word is filtered, to a degree, by your past experiences. You no doubt have said to yourself or others after reading a particular segment of the Bible, "I know that truth in the Bible is real because of what happened to me."

The more we see the Bible as relating to our personal experiences, the more the Bible confirms, encourages, convicts, challenges, affirms, and transforms us. We come to the place where we see that God's Word is universal—applicable to every person in every culture in all ages—as well as highly personal and individualized. There is nothing within the realm of human experience, emotions, and attitudes that the Scriptures fail to address. The Bible is about people and God's relationship to people. The Bible tells us how God works in and through experiences to communicate with people. Certainly as we look back on history, we see that human nature has not changed. The details related to technology or location may change, but the human heart remains the same. What people experienced in Bible times, people also experience today.

Our ability to relate to the Bible does not make the Bible true. The Bible is truth, period. What I am saying is this: The Bible should be our prime source for understanding and interpreting what we experience in life. When it comes to the Lord's return, the Bible should be our first and most authoritative source of study. How people felt in Bible times about the Lord's return relates directly to how we feel about the Lord's return. How people responded in Bible times to the message of the Day of the Lord is how people respond today.

The advantage to noting your experiences is that you gain a new understanding about how God has dealt with you in your own life to bring you to the place where you are today. In reflecting on God's goodness and provision to you, your faith is strengthened to trust God to be with you in the future.

The advantage to sharing your experiences with others as they relate to the Bible is that you grow spiritually when you tell others what God has done for you. You will also find that your personal witness becomes stronger and you'll find that witnessing becomes easier the more you share your experiences in the Lord. Even if you are doing this study on your own, I encourage you to talk to others about your faith experiences.

Emotional Responses

We each have a unique emotional response to God's Word. No one emotional response is more valid or "right" than another. You may feel joy or relief after reading a passage, while the person next to you may be puzzled or frightened at reading the same passage.

Face your emotional responses honestly. Learn to share your emotions with others.

As is the case with experience, emotional responses do not make the Bible true. The value in looking at our emotional responses lies in our gaining greater understanding about what the Lord desires to do in our lives and the ways in which He is using His Word to cause spiritual growth in us.

Let me give you an example of this. If you are reading a passage of the Bible about the second coming of Christ and you feel fear, the question to ask is, "Why, Lord, am I afraid?" Explore your emotional response. What is it that is causing your fear? What are you worried about? An honest look at your own concerns and fears is likely to result in further study directed toward the underlying causes of your fear, and this can produce great healing in you and be of great benefit to you.

We must always recognize that the Bible has an emotional impact on us. We simply cannot read it without having some kind of emotional response to it. Sometimes we are moved to tears by what we read. At other times we may feel great elation, sorrow, hope, longing, surprise, love . . . and yes, even anger and indignation. Allow the Scriptures to touch your heart. God created you with emotions. He knows that you feel certain ways toward Him, toward others, and toward His Word. What He desires is that you be in touch with your feelings. He knows how you feel. He wants *you* to know how you feel, and to explore why you feel what you feel.

As you meet with others, you will find it far more advantageous to a group study to share emotional responses and experiences than to share ideas or opinions. Don't allow yourselves to become sidetracked by opinions of others related to the Lord's return. Speculation and man-concocted theories have no place in a study aimed at learning the truth of God's Word. Scholarly commentaries have their place, but ultimately, the Bible is a spiritual book that reflects the unfathomable riches of God's own Spirit. Emotions are often very close to reflecting a genuine spiritual response.

The topic of the Lord's return is a topic about which many people have very strong opinions, not all of which may be directly related to what the Bible says. Too often, ideas and opinions divide groups. A sharing of emotional responses and experiences, in contrast, tends to unite and to create stronger bonds of community.

Be aware of one particular tendency that may arise in your group. Many who approach topics related to eternity feel a degree of doubt or conviction about their own spiritual state. The tendency of some is to say to those who express doubt or concern, "Don't worry. You'll be all right." That is a wonderful response to give to a person who truly is born again . . . but it is a disastrous response to give to a person who has not truly been saved. Be aware that there may be those in your midst who are not saved or who do not know with certainty that they have been saved. Give them an opportunity to come to Christ as they read and study the Word and the Holy Spirit deals with their hearts. Don't press them to this decision; at the same time, do not deny them the opportunity to experience Christ's salvation of their souls.

Challenges

God always intends for us to be challenged in some way by His Word. He has a purpose in communicating with us—our spiritual growth and transformation into the likeness of Jesus Christ. Since none of us have been fully transformed, we all have room to grow spiritually, and therefore, God will continue to challenge us even though we may have been a born-again believer for many years.

The simple fact is this: Not one of us has done all, said all, or become all that we desire to do, say, or be prior to the Lord's return. We all have more that we would like to do before that day!

Real growth does not come simply by knowing or understanding God's Word, but rather, by applying it to our daily lives and relationships. As you read and study God's Word, identify as best you can specific ways in which you believe God is challenging you, stretching you, or causing you to trust Him in new ways. A topic such as the Lord's return may seem to relate only to your heavenly future. In fact, it is a topic that has direct relevance and application to your life today—in the here and now. What you believe about the Lord's return will have a direct bearing on how you live your life, and especially on how you share the gospel with others.

God desires to get you into His Word for one main purpose—so He can get His Word into you. The Word will change your life, your thinking, your decisions, your outlook. It will also compel you to make changes in your behavior. And increasingly as you grow in the Lord, you will be challenged to share what you know from God's Word with others.

Always be alert for opportunities to discuss the things you are learning in this study. Some of those opportunities may appear suddenly or even seem coincidental. From God's perspective, however, these opportunities are divine appointments. The greater your understanding of God's eternal plan and the importance of salvation, the more of God's truth you will have to share with those who are unsaved, unsure about their salvation, without hope, or wavering in their commitment to follow Christ. Do not be surprised when God brings such people across your path—you have a life-giving, life-changing message to share with them! Be bold in your witness.

If you do not have someone with whom you can discuss your insights, experiences, emotional responses, and challenges, find someone. You may feel led to start a Bible study in your home. You may want to talk to your pastor about organizing a Bible study group in your church. There is much you can learn on your own. There is much more to be learned as you become part of a small group that desires to grow in the Lord and to understand His Word more fully.

Keep the Bible Central

Again, I encourage you to keep the Bible central to your study. Come to God's Word eager to receive all that the Lord desires to impart to you. Come with an insatiable appetite and thirst for the truth.

If you are doing a personal Bible study, be diligent in keeping your focus on God's Word. Remember at all times that gaining insight into the future is not the goal. Becoming more like Jesus Christ, stronger in your witness for Him, and being prepared at all times for His return—these are the goals.

Prayer

Finally, I encourage you to begin and end each Bible study session in prayer. Ask God to give you spiritual eyes to see and spiritual ears to hear what He wants you to see and hear. Ask Him to give you new insights into His Word, bring to your mind experiences that relate to what you read, and to help you identify and clarify your emotions. Ask Him to reveal to you clearly what He desires for you to be, say, and do in response to His Word.

As you end a Bible study session, ask the Lord to plant His Word in your heart so that it might take root, grow, and bear fruit. Ask Him to transform you into the likeness of Jesus Christ. Ask Him to show you ways to apply the Scriptures to your daily life. Pray for the courage to act upon what He is calling you to do.

- *What new insights about the Lord's return do you hope to gain from this study?*

_____

_____

- *Have you struggled in the past with the topic of the Lord's return?*

_____

_____

- *Do you feel comfortable telling others about the Lord's return? Do you feel comfortable telling others about how to prepare for the Lord's return?*

_____

_____

LESSON 2

THE PROMISE OF HIS RETURN

The Lord Jesus Christ has promised that He will return. Of that we can be very certain in the Scriptures.

There are several terms that are important for us to clarify as we begin this study:

Rapture. This refers to a "catching away" of the church prior to the Lord's return. The word *Rapture* does not occur in the New Testament, but it is the word that has been used traditionally by the church from the earliest sermons and commentaries written by Christians. The Rapture is a time when all believers are united with the Lord Jesus Christ prior to His coming again to rule and reign on the earth.

Second Coming and *Millennium.* The "first coming" of Christ was when Jesus, the only begotten Son of God, was born as a baby in Bethlehem. Jesus walked this earth—a real person in a real body, to preach a vibrant message of God's love and forgiveness, to heal and deliver all who came to Him for healing and deliverance, and to die a sacrificial death of atonement on the cross so that mankind could be reconciled fully to God the Father.

The "second coming" of Christ refers to the time when Jesus will return again to the earth, this time as the King of kings and Lord of lords. He will reside on this earth in a physical, *glorified* form, this time to rule and reign over all mankind and all creation. Those who are believers in Christ Jesus will rule and reign with Him.

The reign of Christ on the earth has been described in Revelation 20:6: They "shall reign with Him a thousand years." The "Millennium," a thousand-year period, has been the subject of much debate through the centuries but of this we can be certain: It is a time when Satan will be bound, Christ will be in charge, and the peace that has eluded mankind will prevail.

The Day of the Lord and *the Great Tribulation.* The term "Day of the Lord" is used primarily in the Old Testament and it refers to a day of great judgment on the earth—a day when the wrath of God is poured out on the earth by fire, the earth is purged of all sin, and all who reside on the earth are in total subjugation to an awesome display of the Lord's power.

In Christianity, the "Day of the Lord" has been linked to the Great Tribulation, which is not regarded as an actual *day* but rather a seven-year period of great distress and turmoil. It is a time that ends with the Battle of Armageddon and the return of Jesus to rule and reign on the earth.

The Scriptures that refer to one or more of these events are numerous. We will be able to focus on only a limited number of them in this study. Our purpose in this first lesson is to see what *Jesus* said about His return and about how we are to prepare ourselves.

On the night before His crucifixion, Jesus said to His disciples,

Now the Son of Man is glorified, and God is glorified in Him. If God is glorified in Him, God will also glorify Him in Himself, and glorify Him immediately. Little children, I shall be with you a little while longer. You will seek Me; and as I said to the Jews, "Where I am going, you cannot come," so now I say to you. A new commandment I give to you, that you love one another; as I have loved you, that you also love one another. By this all will know that you are My disciples, if you have love for one another. (John 13:31–35)

Jesus was referring to His death by crucifixion and to the three days that He would be "away" from the disciples (the time between His crucifixion and resurrection). Note that Jesus was most concerned that during this time of His absence, the disciples would "love one another."

- *What new insights do you have into this passage—especially as it relates to how we are to live?*

_____

_____

Simon Peter asked the Lord after He had made this statement, "Lord, where are You going?" Jesus replied, "Where I am going you cannot follow Me now, but you shall follow Me afterward" (see John 13:36). Jesus was again referring to His death. This was not the time for Peter to die, but at the same time, Jesus noted that one day Peter *would* die a similar death.

Peter again said, "Lord, why can I not follow You now? I will lay down my life for Your sake." Jesus answered Peter, "Will you lay down your life for My sake? Most assuredly, I say to you, the rooster shall not crow till you have denied Me three times" (see John 13:37–38). But then, after addressing Peter's boast, Jesus addressed Peter's deep concern and grief. He said,

Let not your heart be troubled; you believe in God, believe also in Me. In My Father's house are many mansions; if it were not so, I would have told you. I go to prepare a place for you. And if I go and prepare a place for you, I will come again and receive you to Myself; that where I am, there you may be also. And where I go you know, and the way you know. (John 14:1–4)

I want you to note five specific things that Jesus said to Peter and His other disciples about this time that He would be away:

1. "Don't let My absence trouble you. Don't worry or be in anguish about My absence."
2. "Believe in Me." In other words, "Trust Me. Recognize that God's plan is unfolding right on schedule."
3. "I am going to prepare a place for you."
4. "I am coming back for you so that you can always be with Me."
5. "You know deep within yourself both where I am going and what it will take for you to be with Me."

These are the same things the Lord says to us today in His absence:

- "Don't be worried by the fact that you can't see Me or that I am away from you."
- "Continue to believe in Me. All things are unfolding just as God our heavenly Father has planned them."

The Lord is preparing a place for us—and what a wonderful place it is going to be! He is going to return and receive us to Himself so that we will never be separated from Him again. We know this will happen, we know where we will one day be, and we know it with certainty because we know how to ensure our relationship with Jesus Christ forever.

- *What new insights do you have into this passage from John 14:1–4?*

_____

_____

- *How do you feel about these words of the Lord?*

_____

_____

Thomas, another of Jesus' disciples, said to the Lord, "Lord, we do not know where You are going, and how can we know the way?" Jesus replied to Thomas, "I am the way, the truth, and the life. No one comes to the Father except through Me" (see John 14:5–6).

As believers in Christ Jesus we can have great confidence in these words of our Lord. He is the way to salvation, He is the full embodiment of God's plan and purpose for mankind, and He is life everlasting. When we accept Jesus as our Savior, we receive God's forgiveness and the Holy Spirit, whom Jesus sends to indwell all who believe in Him. In receiving Jesus, we receive the One who is the way, the truth, and the life. We know the way because we know Christ as our Savior. We know the truth because we have the Holy Spirit within us to convict and convince us of the truth. We know life because the Holy Spirit is eternal and He resides in us—we will live forever because we live in Him and He lives in us.

That is our assurance as we await the Lord's coming. We are going to be with Him forever, regardless of the events that occur between this very moment and the moment we see Christ face-to-face.

If we are alive at the time of the Rapture, we will immediately be with Him. If we die before the Rapture, we will instantly be with the Lord. We will dwell in the place the Lord has prepared for us.

- *How do you feel about the prospect of living with the Lord forever?*

_____

_____

• *What new insights do you have into John 14:5–6?*

_____

_____

What the Word Says	What the Word Says to Me
[Paul said,] "Behold, I tell you a mystery: We shall not all sleep, but we shall all be changed—in a moment, in the twinkling of an eye, at the last trumpet . . . For this corruptible must put on incorruption, and this mortal must put on immortality." (1 Cor. 15:51–53)	_____ _____ _____ _____ _____ _____ _____ _____ _____ _____
[Paul said,] "We are confident, yes, well pleased rather to be absent from the body and to be present with the Lord." (2 Cor. 5:8)	_____ _____ _____ _____ _____

The Uninterrupted Reign of our Lord

One of the most wonderful passages in the Scriptures is a passage that encompasses both Christ's first coming and His second coming:

> For unto us a Child is born,
> Unto us a Son is given;
> And the government will be upon His shoulder.
> And His name will be called
> Wonderful, Counselor, Mighty God,
> Everlasting Father, Prince of Peace.

Of the increase of His government and peace
There will be no end,
Upon the throne of David and over His kingdom,
To order it and establish it with judgment and justice
From that time forward, even forever.
The zeal of the LORD of hosts will perform this. (Isa.
9:6–7)

This passage refers to an important concept related to the Lord's return: We are all subject to the Lord's rulership. Not all people on the earth have accepted that fact—not all acknowledge Jesus as Savior and Lord. Nonetheless, from the moment Jesus was born, He instituted "active rulership" over this world. No powers of darkness could prevail over Him during His earthly life, and no powers of darkness can or will prevail over Him now or ever. The uninterrupted reign of Jesus has already begun! Jesus sits at the right hand of God the Father today to "order" and "establish" His kingdom with "judgment and justice." His will is being done on this earth even now, regardless of our ability to perceive it or recognize it.

What we also see in this passage is the truth that the "increase of His government and peace" will continue with "no end." The Lord Jesus is not losing power the longer He delays His return to the earth. He is increasing His rulership over the earth. With every sinner who comes to Him, Jesus increases His government and peace. With every victory over the enemy—which may be a victory of healing, deliverance, or salvation—the Lord extends His justice and righteousness.

The rulership of the Lord will continue without interruption until the day when we are all with the Lord. And what a great and glorious time that will be!

• *What new insights do you have into Isaiah 9:6–7?*

_____

_____

- *In your walk with the Lord, have you experienced an increase in the Lord's rulership over your life—an increase in His standards of righteousness and His peace? Cite specific examples.*

What the Word Says	**What the Word Says to Me**
Then the angel [Gabriel] said to her [Mary], "Do not be afraid, Mary, for you have found favor with God. And behold, you will conceive in your womb and bring forth a Son, and shall call His name JESUS. He will be great, and will be called the Son of the Highest; and the Lord God will give Him the throne of His father David. And He will reign over the house of Jacob forever, and of His kingdom there will be no end." (Luke 1:30–33)	------------------------------------
For I consider that the sufferings of this present time are not worthy to be compared with the glory which shall be revealed in us. For the earnest expectation of the creation eagerly waits for the revealing of the sons of God. For the creation was subjected to	------------------------------------

futility, not willingly, but because of Him who subjected it in hope; because the creation itself also will be delivered from the bondage of corruption into the glorious liberty of the children of God. For we know that the whole creation groans and labors with birth pangs together until now. And not only they, but we also who have the firstfruits of the Spirit, even we ourselves groan within ourselves, eagerly waiting for the adoption, the redemption of our body. For we were saved in this hope . . . we eagerly wait for it with perseverance. (Rom. 8:18–25)

Our Agenda as Believers

As Jesus was preparing to ascend to the Father, He told His disciples to stay in Jerusalem to await the coming of the "Promise" of the Father, the Holy Spirit. He said, "You have heard from Me; for John truly baptized with water, but you shall be baptized with the Holy Spirit not many days from now" (Acts 1:4–5). The disciples asked Him, "Lord, will You at this time restore the kingdom to Israel?" (Acts 1:6) Read closely what Jesus said to them:

> It is not for you to know times or seasons which the Father has put in His own authority. But you shall receive power when the Holy Spirit has come upon you; and you shall be witnesses to Me in Jerusalem, and in

all Judea and Samaria, and to the end of the earth. (Acts 1:7–8)

Jesus made it very clear what we as believers in Him are to be doing until He returns and "receives" us to Himself:

- We are to receive the power of the Holy Spirit into our lives. We are to yield ourselves daily to the Holy Spirit, asking the Holy Spirit to direct our steps into God's perfect will for our lives.
- We are to be His witnesses "to the end of the earth." We are to share the Gospel of Jesus Christ with every person possible prior to the Lord's return or our death, whichever comes first.

That is our agenda as believers!

- *What new insights do you have into Acts 1:7–8?*

_____

_____

- *Reflect upon your personal experience in receiving the power of the Holy Spirit and being His witness.*

_____

_____

- *How do you feel about the Lord's challenge to be His "witness" to the end of the earth?*

_____

_____

The Literal Return of Christ

As Jesus was taken up and a "cloud" received Him out of the sight of the disciples who were gathered with Him on the Mount of Olives, the Bible tells us that "two men stood by them in white apparel, who also said, 'Men of Galilee, why do you stand gazing up into heaven? This same Jesus, who was taken up from you into heaven, will so come in like manner as you saw Him go into heaven'" (Acts 1:10–11).

In the manner that Jesus departed, He will return. His ascension was literal; His return will be literal. His ascension was in bodily form; His return will be in bodily form.

The second coming of the Lord will not be a coming in "spirit" or a coming in "idea" or a coming in "miracles"—it will be a real coming, just as His ascension was a real going.

- *What new insights do you have into Acts 1:10–11?*

_____

_____

What the Word Says

[Jesus said,] "If they say to you, 'Look, He is in the desert!' do not go out; or 'Look, He is in the inner rooms!' do not believe it. For as the lightning comes from the east and flashes to the west, so also will the coming of the Son of Man be." (Matt. 24:26–27)

[Jesus said to the high priest,] "It is as you said. Nevertheless, I say to you, hereafter you will see the Son of Man sitting at the right hand of the Power, and coming on the clouds of heaven." (Matt. 26:64)

What the Word Says to Me

[Jesus said,] "Then they will see the Son of Man coming in the clouds with great power and glory." (Mark 13:26)

Behold, He is coming with clouds, and every eye will see Him, even they who pierced Him. And all the tribes of the earth will mourn because of Him. (Rev. 1:7)

Yes, the Lord is coming again! The question we each must ask ourselves is this: Am I doing the things that the Lord has told me to do until that day? Am I doing all I can do to be ready for His return?

- *What new insights do you have into the Lord's return?*

- *In what specific ways is the Lord challenging you today in your spirit?*

LESSON 3

GOD'S MAGNIFICENT MASTER PLAN

God has a magnificent master plan for His creation. It is a plan that has been in place since the beginning of time. It is a plan that is unfolding just as God intended it to unfold.

One of the most beneficial ways we can look at the second coming of Christ is to approach it by looking at His first coming. We see in the first coming an amazing series of events and prophecies woven together in precision and culminating in the birth of Jesus.

The Lord "prepared" the world for the birth of Jesus in four main ways:

1. Spoken prophecies
2. Symbols and prophetic signs
3. Sovereign provision for and preparation of His people
4. Sovereign rule over nations and nature

As He prepared the world for the first coming, so He will prepare the world for the Second Coming.

Proclamations of the Prophets

God spoke repeatedly through His prophets about the coming of the Messiah, Jesus Christ, His Only begotten Son. The first prophecy is one that is often overlooked, but it is one that also has bearing on the second coming of the Lord. It was a word of the Lord to the serpent that deceived Eve:

> And I will put enmity
> Between you and the woman,
> And between your seed and her Seed;
> He shall bruise your head,
> And you shall bruise His heel. (Gen. 3:15)

Eve's "Seed" was Jesus, her heir. Satan was allowed to "bruise" the heel of Jesus—a bruising that was an annoyance. Jesus, in contrast, will bruise Satan's head—utterly destroying his power, authority, and influence. The bruise to the head of Satan will mean a total defeat.

We must never lose sight of the fact that Jesus came to destroy the works of the devil. He came to win back what the devil tried to steal from God. He came back to defeat the devil at every turn. What Jesus began at the Cross, He continues to do by the power of His Holy Spirit in human lives today. The work of Jesus in defeating the devil is ongoing.

The purpose of Christ's coming as our Savior was to destroy the devil's authority and power over our spirits, souls, and bodies; Jesus came to restore man to God. In His second coming, Christ will restore all of creation and all of the world's systems to God in both the spiritual and natural realms.

What the Word Says	What the Word Says to Me
[Jesus said,] "The thief does not come except to steal, and to kill, and to destroy. I have come that they may have life,	-----------------------------------

and that they may have it more
abundantly." (John 10:10)

[Jesus said,] "The Son of Man
has come to seek and to save
that which was lost." (Luke
19:10)

- *What new insights do you have into the reason for Christ's coming?*

- *Can you cite an experience or an instance in which you knew with certainty that the Lord has defeated the work of Satan in your life?*

A number of other prophecies in the Old Testament refer to
the specifics of Christ's birth, life, and death. Through the ages,
our heavenly Father made known His plans for the birth of His
Son. The Lord is no less precise in His plans and preparation
for the second coming of Christ. Following are three prophecies related to Christ's birth, and three related to His return.
Just as the prophecies related to Christ's birth have been fulfilled with precision, so we can expect the prophecies related
to Christ's return to be fulfilled in detail.

What the Word Says	What the Word Says to Me
But you, Bethlehem Ephrathah, Though you are little among the thousands of Judah,	

Yet out of you shall come forth
to Me
The One to be Ruler in Israel,
Whose goings forth are from of
old,
From everlasting. (Mic. 5:2)

Rejoice greatly, O daughter of
Zion!
Shout, O daughter of
Jerusalem!
Behold, your King is coming
to you;
He is just and having salvation,
Lowly and riding on a donkey,
A colt, the foal of a donkey.
(Zech. 9:9)

Therefore the Lord Himself
will give you a sign: Behold,
the virgin shall conceive and
bear a Son, and shall call His
name Immanuel. (Isa. 7:14)

Now the Spirit expressly says
that in latter times some will
depart from the faith, giving
heed to deceiving spirits and
doctrines of demons, speaking
lies in hypocrisy, having their
own conscience seared with a
hot iron, forbidding to marry,
and commanding to abstain
from foods which God cre-
ated to be received with

thanksgiving by those who believe and know the truth. (1 Tim. 4:1–3)

But know this, that in the last days perilous times will come: For men will be lovers of themselves, lovers of money, boasters, proud, blasphemers, disobedient to parents, unthankful, unholy, unloving, unforgiving, slanderers, without self-control, brutal, despisers of good, traitors, headstrong, haughty, lovers of pleasure rather than lovers of God, having a form of godliness but denying its power. (2 Tim. 3:1–5)

For the time will come when they will not endure sound doctrine, but according to their own desires, because they have itching ears, they will heap up for themselves teachers; and they will turn their ears away from the truth, and be turned aside to fables. But you be watchful in all things, endure afflictions, do the work of an evangelist, fulfill your ministry. (2 Tim. 4:3–5)

Symbols and Prophetic Signs

One of the ways in which the Lord foretold the coming of Jesus, and the *nature* of the Messiah, was through signs and symbols.

One of the foremost symbols is that of the shed blood of a lamb. Throughout the Old Testament, we find the shedding of the blood of a lamb to be associated with the forgiveness of sins. In the Garden of Eden, God covered Adam and Eve with "skins"—the implication is that an innocent animal was slain by God to provide a "covering" for Adam and Eve, a covering that reminded them continually of the fact that their sin would result in a physical death. Later, God instituted animal sacrifices for the remission of sin and as a "blood covering" against death (especially at Passover and the Day of Atonement). The necessity for blood sacrifices ended with the blood sacrifice of Jesus on the cross.

Another "sign" that was used in a prophetic way by God was the crossing of the Red Sea. The passage of God's people through the water was a sign of baptism to come. The "sign" of a pillar of cloud by day and of fire by night that led the Israelites through the wilderness was a prophetic sign that God would send His Spirit to lead His people to the fulfillment of all His promises.

Jesus made reference to an Old Testament sign as being prophetic of His crucifixion. (See the following passages.)

Now it is important to recognize that the people to whom these signs were given did not understand their full importance. The signs were recognized by them as acts of deliverance, healing, and help. In like manner, we may not understand the full significance of the signs prophesied in the New Testament about the coming of the Lord. They will be understood by us, however, in the same way the signs of old were understood—we will perceive them as signs of the Lord's deliverance, healing, and help.

One of the signs that Jesus gave as an indicator of His coming and the end of the age is given in Matthew 24:4–8 which follows. How will we receive this sign? What is our response to be?

What the Word Says

Then the LORD said to Moses, "Make a fiery serpent, and set it on a pole; and it shall be that everyone who is bitten, when he looks at it, shall live." So Moses made a bronze serpent, and put it on a pole; and so it was, if a serpent had bitten anyone, when he looked at the bronze serpent, he lived. (Num. 21:8–9)

[Jesus said,] "As Moses lifted up the serpent in the wilderness, even so must the Son of Man be lifted up, that whoever believes in Him should not perish but have eternal life." (John 3:14–15)

[Jesus said,] "Take heed that no one deceives you. For many will come in My name, saying, 'I am the Christ,' and will deceive many. And you will hear of wars and rumors of wars. See that you are not troubled; for all these things must come to pass, but the

What the Word Says to Me

----

end is not yet. For nation will rise against nation, and kingdom against kingdom. And there will be famines, pestilences, and earthquakes in various places. All these are the beginning of sorrows." (Matt. 24:4–8)

Sovereign Provision for and Protection of God's People

If we take the entire Old Testament as a whole, we find countless stories that, taken together, reveal God's divine protection and provision for "His elect." God's people were sovereignly guided, spared, guarded, and nurtured as part of God's plan to teach and prepare His people for the Messiah. He worked as a Great Shepherd, guiding His sheep across arid ground and dangerous ravines until He brought them to a place of green pastures and still waters.

- *Read Nehemiah 9:5–33. What new insights do you have into God's sovereign rule over His people?*

_____

_____

Slowly over time, bit by bit, the Lord revealed Himself to His people. He imparted facets of His name as He revealed His character. He performed miracles and issued specific prophecies to reveal His purposes.

As you read through some of the names of God below, consider the many ways in which God revealed Himself to the Israelites as a means of teaching them about Himself, and as a means of preparing them for Jesus.

Name	*Meaning*
Abba	Father
Shaddai	Almighty
El Olam	Everlasting God
Elohim	Creator
El Roi	The One who responds to need
Qedosh Yisrael	The Holy God, set apart for Israel
Adonai	Master, Lord
YHWH	Personal Lord
YHWH-Nissi	The Lord who protects me
YHWH-Sabaoth	The Lord of hosts (armies)
YHWH-Shalom	The Lord of peace
YHWH-Yireh	The Lord who provides
YHWH-Tsidkenu	The righteous Lord
YHWH-Rohi	The Lord who is the Shepherd of loving care

• *What new insights do you have into the sovereign nature of God in protecting and providing for His people as He prepared them for the first coming of Jesus?*

_____

_____

Now consider some of the names that have been given to Jesus. How do they prepare and teach us about the Lord's nature and character—not only now, but in His coming again?

Name	*Meaning*
Alpha and Omega	Beginning and Ending
Bread of Life	Essential for life
Chief Cornerstone	The sure foundation

High Priest	Our mediator
Immanuel	"God with us"—the One who always stands with us
Jesus	"Yahweh saves"
King of kings, Lord of lords	The sovereign almighty
Lamb of God	The One who offers His life as a sacrifice for sin
Rabbi	Teacher
Shepherd	The One who gives guidance and protection
Word	God's supreme communication to mankind

- *What new insights do you have into the role that Jesus plays in our lives today as He prepares us for His return?*

_____

_____

- *Reflect over your life. Are there times when you seemed to "learn" one of the names of God or Jesus in a more personal way?*

_____

_____

Sovereign Rule of Nations and Nature

The Lord does not only govern His people and prepare them for the fulfillment of His plan and purposes, but He governs all nations and all of nature.

Many Bible scholars refer to the four-hundred-year span between Malachi and Matthew as the "silent years." God was anything but inactive during this time. It was during these four hundred years that Alexander the Great conquered the nations around the Mediterranean and united the world under the

Greek language. It was during this period that the Greek Bible was written (Septuagint), which was a great force in the evangelism of the Gentile world after the crucifixion of Jesus.

God used the Romans to build good roads, institute free and open travel, and allow for the coexistence of "many religions"—all of which were factors that enhanced the spread of the gospel during the first century. It was a Roman census that brought Joseph and Mary to Bethlehem for the birth of Jesus, in fulfillment of prophecy. It was Roman crucifixion that provided the means for Christ's death as one "lifted up" for the salvation of mankind.

On the night that Jesus was born, God arranged for a new star to appear in the heavens—a star that was a signal to the wise men to bring their gifts that would honor Jesus as our Messiah (prophet, priest, and king).

Throughout the ages, God was doing His great and mighty work. If God could so arrange the history of the nations and the course of nature in anticipation of the birth of Jesus, surely He is at work arranging the history of nations and the course of nature in anticipation of Christ's return.

What the Word Says	What the Word Says to Me
You alone are the LORD;	
You have made heaven,	
The heaven of heavens, with	
all their host,	
The earth and everything on it,	
The seas and all that is in	
them,	
And You preserve them all.	
The host of heaven worships	
You. (Neh. 9:6)	
In the beginning was the Word,	
and the Word was with God,	

and the Word was God. He was in the beginning with God. All things were made through Him, and without Him nothing was made that was made. (John 1:1–3)

The LORD is high above all nations. (Ps. 113:4)

We also are men with the same nature as you, and preach to you that you should turn from these useless things to the living God, who made the heaven, the earth, the sea, and all things that are in them, who in bygone generations allowed all nations to walk in their own ways. Nevertheless He did not leave Himself without witness, in that He did good, gave us rain from heaven and fruitful seasons, filling our hearts with food and gladness. (Acts 14:15–17)

He is before all things, and in Him all things consist. (Col. 1:17)

God's preparation is meticulous. He leaves no detail unattended or unfinished. His plan for mankind through the ages is unfolding just as He designed it to unfold. There are no surprises, no detours, no delays.

We can trust God's plan. We can trust God's promises regarding His people and about the Lord's return to be true. He is utterly faithful to His Word and to those who believe it.

• *What new insights do you have into the return of the Lord?*

_____

_____

• *How do you feel, knowing that God has a master plan for your life and for all mankind?*

_____

_____

• *In what ways are you feeling challenged in your spirit?*

_____

_____

LESSON 4

IN THE FULLNESS OF TIME

The question that most people ask about the second coming of Christ is this: "When will it be?" Jesus' own disciples asked this question of the Lord. They said to Jesus privately, "Tell us, when will these things be?" (Matt. 24:3).

Jesus gave them several general signs that would indicate the time was approaching, but then He gave this statement:

> Of that day and hour no one knows, not even the angels of heaven, but My Father only. But as the days of Noah were, so also will the coming of the Son of Man be. For as in the days before the flood, they were eating and drinking, marrying and giving in marriage, until the day that Noah entered the ark, and did not know until the flood came and took them all away, so also will the coming of the Son of Man be . . . Watch therefore, for you do not know what hour your Lord is coming. (Matt. 24:36–39, 42)

- *What new insights do you have into this passage?*

_____

_____

- *How do you feel about the fact that no person will know the day and hour of Christ's return?*

_____

_____

- *Thinking back over your life, recall a time when you wanted to know when something was going to happen, but that information was withheld from you? What did you do? What was the outcome?*

_____

_____

No matter what any person may calculate from the Scriptures, we will not know the day and hour of Christ's coming. Only the Father has that information.

There are several things, however, of which we can be certain and it is on those things that we will focus in this lesson.

God's Timing Is Perfect

God did not send Jesus to the earth the first time without preparation that included an absolute perfection in timing. Neither will Jesus return to the earth without preparation and perfect timing.

The fact is, however, that God's timing is not always our timing. God's ways are not our ways. As we read in Isaiah,

> "My thoughts are not your thoughts,
> Nor are your ways My ways," says the LORD.
> "For as the heavens are higher than the earth,
> So are My ways higher than your ways,
> And My thoughts than your thoughts." (55:8–9)

What we count on is that God will send His Son back to this earth in the perfection of His timing, not necessarily in the timing that we desire.

One of the concepts we find repeatedly in the Scriptures is that of the "fullness of time." Paul wrote to the Galatians that God sent Jesus to the earth as our Savior in "the fullness of the time" (Gal. 4:4). The fullness of the time refers to the perfection of timing. All things are in place, all prerequisites have been completed, all things are *ready*.

A normal, healthy baby is born not according to a calendar or a physician's predictions, but in the fullness of time—the right time for that baby to be born.

God sees things from a perspective of eternity. He is not locked into time as we are. He sees precisely the right moment when all things are in place according to His plan, and in that split moment, He acts. The apostle Paul wrote to Timothy, "Keep this commandment without spot, blameless until our Lord Jesus Christ's appearing, which He will manifest in His own time, He who is the blessed and only Potentate, the King of kings and Lord of lords, who alone has immortality, dwelling in unapproachable light" (1 Tim. 6:14–16).

Perhaps the best answer we can ever give about *when* the Lord will come again is this: When the time is right according to God the Father.

What the Word Says	What the Word Says to Me
But when the fullness of the time had come, God sent forth His Son, born of a woman, born under the law, to redeem those who were under the law, that we might receive the adoption as sons. (Gal. 4:4–5)	-------------------------------------
In the dispensation of the fullness of the times He might gather together in one all things in Christ, both which	-------------------------------------

are in heaven and which are on earth—in Him. (Eph. 1:10)

Repent therefore and be converted, that your sins may be blotted out, so that times of refreshing may come from the presence of the Lord, and that He may send Jesus Christ, who was preached to you before, whom heaven must receive until the times of restoration of all things, which God has spoken by the mouth of all His holy prophets since the world began. (Acts 3:19–21)

Times are not hidden from the Almighty. (Job 24:1)

But as for me, I trust in You, O LORD; I say, "You are my God." My times are in Your hand. (Ps. 31:14–15)

The Character of the End Times

If we cannot know the precise timing of the Lord's return, what *can* we know about God's timing? We can know with certainty three things related to timing: We will be able to discern the signs associated with the coming of the Lord as they happen, we will have a sense that the time is drawing close, and, we are to be ready at all times. (We will deal with only the first of these three signs in this lesson and the remaining two in the next lesson.)

Discerning the Signs as They Happen

We will have an understanding of end-time events as they happen. Many people desire to predict future events in the light of current events, but this is not the pattern given to us in the Scriptures. Rather, we will have an understanding of events as they occur. Jesus said to the Pharisees who asked Him to show them a sign from heaven:

> When it is evening you say, "It will be fair weather, for the sky is red"; and in the morning, "It will be foul weather today, for the sky is red and threatening." Hypocrites! You know how to discern the face of the sky, but you cannot discern the signs of the times. A wicked and adulterous generation seeks after a sign, and no sign shall be given to it except the sign of the prophet Jonah. (Matt. 16:2–4)

Jesus was referring to the "signs" surrounding His death and resurrection. The sign of the prophet Jonah was not understood until the Resurrection. There were many things that Jesus said and did that His closest disciples did not understand until after Jesus was crucified and rose from the dead. John wrote this about the fulfillment of the prophecy concerning Jesus' riding into Jerusalem on a donkey's colt: "His disciples did not understand these things at first; but when Jesus was glorified, then they remembered that these things were written about Him and that they had done these things to Him" (John 12:16).

> • *Recall an incident in your life in which you understood something clearly as it happened or after it happened, but had no full understanding about it prior to its happening.*

Also note this statement from Matthew 16:4: "A wicked and adulterous generation seeks after a sign, and no sign shall be given to it." The world is not going to be able to discern the spiritual signs of God at work. That was true then; it is true now. We must have spiritual eyes and spiritual ears in order to discern spiritual matters. Discernment is the function of the Holy Spirit in our lives.

What is it that Jesus told His disciples to discern? In Matthew 24, Jesus began His explanation of future events in this way:

> Take heed that no one deceives you. For many will come in My name, saying, "I am the Christ," and will deceive many. And you will hear of wars and rumors of wars. See that you are not troubled; for all these things must come to pass, but the end is not yet. For nation will rise against nation, and kingdom against kingdom. And there will be famines, pestilences, and earthquakes in various places. All these are the beginning of sorrows. Then they will deliver you up to tribulation and kill you, and you will be hated by all nations for My name's sake. And then many will be offended, will betray one another, and will hate one another. Then many false prophets will rise up and deceive many. And because lawlessness will abound, the love of many will grow cold. But he who endures to the end shall be saved. And this gospel of the kingdom will be preached in all the world as a witness to all the nations, and then the end will come. (Matt. 24:4–14)

• *What new insights do you have into this passage?*

_____

_____

We included part of this passage in a previous lesson but I want to point out four things to you that are very important as we await the coming of Christ:

First, Jesus warned against deception. He said, "Take heed that no one deceives you." Deceit is a subtle form of lying—it is twisting the truth so that it is nearly impossible to tell truth from lie. As believers in Christ, we are to stand against deceit at all times, quick to speak the Word of God's truth.

What the Word Says

The great dragon was cast out, that serpent of old, called the Devil and Satan, who deceives the whole world. (Rev. 12:9)

For many deceivers have gone out into the world who do not confess Jesus Christ as coming in the flesh. This is a deceiver and an antichrist. (2 John 7)

[Jesus said to the Pharisees,] "You are of your father the devil, and the desires of your father you want to do. He was a murderer from the beginning, and does not stand in the truth, because there is no truth in him. When he speaks a lie, he speaks from his own resources, for he is a liar and the father of it." (John 8:44)

[Jesus said,] "If you abide in My word, you are My disciples indeed. And you shall know the truth, and the truth shall

What the Word Says to Me

_____
_____
_____
_____

_____
_____
_____
_____
_____

_____
_____
_____
_____
_____
_____
_____
_____
_____
_____

_____
_____
_____
_____

make you free." (John
8:31–32)

Second, Jesus foretold a time of great confusion—a time of offense, betrayal, hate, false prophets, and lawlessness. As believers in Christ, we are to display the very opposite traits: loyalty to Christ and to other believers, love, truthful teaching, and law-abiding behavior. We are to be agents of peace.

What the Word Says	**What the Word Says to Me**
God is not the author of confusion but of peace, as in all the churches of the saints. (1 Cor. 14:33)	-------------------------------
For where envy and self-seeking exist, confusion and every evil thing are there. But the wisdom that is from above is first pure, then peaceable, gentle, willing to yield, full of mercy and good fruits, without partiality and without hypocrisy. (James 3:16–17)	-------------------------------

Third, Jesus called for endurance. He said, "He who endures to the end shall be saved" (Matt. 24:13). We are to persevere in what we know to be true and in those works that we know to be righteous.

What the Word Says	**What the Word Says to Me**
[Love] hopes all things, endures all things. (1 Cor. 13:7)	-------------------------------

Blessed is the man who endures temptation; for when he has been approved, he will receive the crown of life which the Lord has promised to those who love Him. (James 1:12)

Then He spoke a parable to them, that men always ought to pray and not lose heart, saying: "There was in a certain city a judge who did not fear God nor regard man. Now there was a widow in that city; and she came to him, saying, 'Get justice for me from my adversary.' And he would not for a while; but afterward he said within himself, 'Though I do not fear God nor regard man, yet because this widow troubles me I will avenge her, lest by her continual coming she weary me.'" Then the Lord said, "Hear what the unjust judge said. And shall God not avenge His own elect who cry out day and night to Him, though He bears long with them? I tell you that He will avenge them speedily. Nevertheless, when the Son of Man comes, will He really find faith on the earth?" (Luke 18:1–8)

Fourth, Jesus spoke of the gospel being preached in all the world as a witness to all nations. We are to share the gospel with as many people as possible, individually in our personal witness and joining with others to reach those in far-away places who still have not heard about Jesus.

What the Word Says	What the Word Says to Me
[Jesus said,] "Go into all the world and preach the gospel to every creature." (Mark 16:15)	
[Jesus said,] "You shall receive power when the Holy Spirit has come upon you; and you shall be witnesses to Me in Jerusalem, and in all Judea and Samaria, and to the end of the earth." (Acts 1:8)	
Walk in wisdom toward those who are outside, redeeming the time. Let your speech always be with grace, seasoned with salt, that you may know how you ought to answer each one. (Col. 4:5–6)	

Each of these four things about which Jesus spoke are things that call us to action today! We are to guard ourselves against deception, staying in the Word so that we will have a clear understanding of right and wrong. We are to trust the Holy Spirit for discernment, truth, guidance, wise counsel, and peace—it is the Holy Spirit who establishes order and unity of spirit. We are to endure, steadfast in our faith and persistent in our good works. And, we are to do our utmost to get the gospel to all the world as a witness to all nations.

We have our marching orders! The signs of the times around us may be terrifying, but if we remain focused on the things we are to be doing in the midst of confusing, lawless, and troubled times, we will be in obedience to the Lord's commands and we will know His salvation.

We may not know the precise time of the Lord's coming, but we *do* know from God's Word what we are to be doing with our time! We know what we are to be doing as the signs of His coming unfold around us.

* *How do you feel about what the Lord has predicted concerning what we are to do in preparing for His return?*

_____

_____

What the Word Says	**What the Word Says to Me**
What manner of persons ought you to be in holy conduct and godliness, looking for and hastening the coming of the day of God . . . ? Nevertheless we, according to His promise, look for new heavens and a new earth in which righteousness dwells. Therefore, beloved, looking forward to these things, be diligent to be found by Him in peace, without spot and blameless. (2 Peter 3:11–14)	_____ _____ _____ _____ _____ _____ _____ _____ _____ _____ _____ _____

See then that you walk circum-
spectly, not as fools but as
wise, redeeming the time,
because the days are evil.
(Eph. 5:15–16)

- *What new insights do you have about preparing for the Lord's coming?*

- *In what ways are you feeling challenged in your spirit?*

AN IMMINENT SURPRISE

The coming of the Lord is going to be, to a very great extent, a *surprise*—a welcome, joyous, glorious surprise—not only to the world at large, but to those who are believers in Christ Jesus. The Christian's approach to this surprise is very different, however, from that of nonbelievers. We who have accepted Jesus as our Savior are to be expecting this surprise, even to the extent of feeling a great urgency in our expectancy, because we hold to a belief that the surprise is imminent, which means very soon or close at hand.

- *How do you feel about surprises in general? How do you feel about a surprise if you know it is going to be a "good" surprise?*

_____

_____

A Joyous Surprise

Jesus made a number of statements about the "surprise" element of His return. He said,

Then two men will be in the field: one will be taken and the other left. Two women will be grinding at the mill: one will be taken and the other left. Watch therefore, for you do not know what hour your Lord is coming. But know this, that if the master of the house had known what hour the thief would come, he would have watched and not allowed his house to be broken into. Therefore you also be ready, for the Son of Man is coming at an hour when you do not expect. (Matt. 24:40–44)

• *What insights do you have into this passage?*

_____

_____

Earlier in this same chapter of Matthew, Jesus had said that life would be "as the days of Noah" at His return. People would be eating, drinking, and getting married—life as usual, all things seemingly "normal." His coming would be a great surprise, just as it was to those who were not aware of what was happening until Noah entered the ark and the floodwaters began to rise.

The coming of the Lord will be without a sounded alarm, without warning sirens, without an opportunity to utter the words "I believe in Christ Jesus." It will be a coming that is swift and immediate.

A Constant State of Readiness

What is to be our response to the fact that the Lord's return is an imminent surprise? We are to be ready. Indeed, we are to live in a constant state of readiness for that moment. Jesus said,

Take heed, watch and pray; for you do not know when the time is. It is like a man going to a far country, who left his house and gave authority to his servants, and to each his work, and commanded the doorkeeper to watch. Watch therefore, for you do not know when the master of the house is coming—in the evening, at midnight, at the crowing of the rooster, or in the morning—lest, coming suddenly, he find you sleeping. And what I say to you, I say to all: Watch! (Mark 13:33–37)

• *What insights do you have into this passage from Mark?*

_____

_____

What the Word Says

[Jesus said,] "Who then is a faithful and wise servant, whom his master made ruler over his household, to give them food in due season? Blessed is that servant whom his master, when he comes, will find so doing. Assuredly, I say to you that he will make him ruler over all his goods. But if that evil servant says in his heart, 'My master is delaying his coming,' and begins to beat his fellow servants, and to eat and drink with the drunkards, the master of that servant will come on a day when he is not looking for him and at an hour that he is not aware of, and will cut him in two and appoint him his portion with the hypocrites. There shall be

What the Word Says to Me

_____

_____

_____

_____

_____

_____

_____

_____

_____

_____

_____

_____

_____

_____

_____

_____

_____

_____

_____

_____

weeping and gnashing of teeth." (Matt. 24:45–51)

[Jesus said,] "But take heed to yourselves, lest your hearts be weighed down with carousing, drunkenness, and cares of this life, and that Day come on you unexpectedly. For it will come as a snare on all those who dwell on the face of the whole earth. Watch therefore, and pray always that you may be counted worthy to escape all these things that will come to pass, and to stand before the Son of Man." (Luke 21:34–36)

Watch and pray. Note in the preceding passage from Luke 21 that the Lord tells His disciples to watch and *pray.* We are to be petitioning God as we await the Lord's coming. And what is it that we are to be petitioning?

On the night of His betrayal as Jesus prayed in the Garden of Gethsemane, He said to His disciple Simon, "I have prayed for you, that your faith should not fail" (Luke 22:32). Surely we need to have this same prayer for ourselves—that our faith will not fail.

We must pray that we will not give in to temptation. Jesus said to His disciples, "Pray that you may not enter into temptation" (Luke 22:40).

We must pray that we will not be deceived. Jesus warned, "False christs and false prophets will rise and show signs and wonders to deceive, if possible, even the elect" (Mark 13:22). We must pray for discernment and an absolute understanding of right and wrong.

We must pray that those of us who are in Christ will continue to love one another and to fulfill Christ's commandments. As you read through the final prayer of Jesus for His disciples, make this prayer your own. Personalize it for yourself and your family:

Father, the hour has come. Glorify Your Son, that Your Son also may glorify You, as You have given Him authority over all flesh, that He should give eternal life to as many as You have given Him. And this is eternal life, that they may know You, the only true God, and Jesus Christ whom You have sent. I have glorified You on the earth. I have finished the work which You have given Me to do. And now, O Father, glorify Me together with Yourself, with the glory which I had with You before the world was. I have manifested Your name to the men whom You have given Me out of the world. They were Yours, You gave them to Me, and they have kept Your word. Now they have known that all things which You have given Me are from You. For I have given to them the words which You have given Me; and they have received them, and have known surely that I came forth from You; and they have believed that You sent Me.

I pray for them. I do not pray for the world but for those whom You have given Me, for they are Yours. And all Mine are Yours, and Yours are Mine, and I am glorified in them. Now I am no longer in the world, but these are in the world, and I come to You. Holy Father, keep through Your name those whom You have given Me, that they may be one as We are. While I was with them in the world, I kept them in Your name. Those whom You gave Me I have kept; and none of them is lost except the son of perdition, that the Scripture might be fulfilled. But now I come to You, and these things I speak in the world, that they may have My joy fulfilled in themselves. I have given them Your word; and the world has hated them because they are not of the world, just as I am not of the world. I do not pray that You should take them out of the world, but that You should keep them from the evil one. They are not of the world, just as I am not of the world. Sanctify them by Your truth. Your word is truth. As You sent Me into the world, I also have sent them into the world. And for their sakes I sanctify Myself, that they also may be sanctified by the truth. I do not pray for these alone, but also for those who will believe in Me through their word; that they all may be one, as You, Father, are in Me, and I in You; that they also may be one in Us, that the world may believe that You sent Me. And the glory which You gave Me I have given them, that they may be one just as We are one: I in them, and You in Me; that they may be made perfect in one, and that the world may know that You have sent Me, and have loved them as You have loved Me. (John 17:1–23)

- *What new insights do you have into this prayer of Jesus and the way in which we are to be praying as we await Christ's coming?*

What the Word Says	What the Word Says to Me
Continue earnestly in prayer, being vigilant in it with thanksgiving. (Col. 4:2)	
Watch and pray, lest you enter into temptation. The spirit indeed is willing, but the flesh is weak. (Mark 14:38)	
Take up the whole armor of God, that you may be able to	

withstand in the evil day, and
having done all, to stand.
Stand therefore . . . praying
always with all prayer and supplication in the Spirit, being
watchful to this end with all
perseverance and supplication
for all the saints. (Eph.
6:13–14, 18)

An active, expectant watch. To "watch" means to be actively looking. It is expectant watching. Jesus gave a number of signs that would precede His coming and then He spoke this parable to His disciples:

> Look at the fig tree, and all the trees. When they are already budding, you see and know for yourselves that summer is now near. So you also, when you see these things happening, know that the kingdom of God is near. Assuredly, I say to you, this generation will by no means pass away till all things take place. Heaven and earth will pass away, but My words will by no means pass away. (Luke 21:29–33)

I want you to note three things in this brief passage.

First, Jesus knew what all men in Israel knew at that time— a budding tree was a sign of spring. Fruit was going to be produced, a harvest was coming. We are to be looking for signs of harvest.

Now for a harvest to be produced, a seed must first be planted and cultivated. A tree must be planted, pruned, trained up, watered, nurtured . . . it is a healthy tree that produces fruit. As we await the coming of the Lord, we are to be about "fruit production." We are to be planting seeds of the gospel in fertile soil, nurturing the spiritual growth of others, and bearing fruit of the Spirit in anticipation of Christ's return. We are to be looking for fruit—expecting revival, and working toward it.

Second, Jesus said that the people who saw these preliminary signs of His coming would know that the kingdom of God was coming within a generation. A generation is several decades—in Scripture, it is usually a period of forty years. Again, we have confirmation that we will not know the day, hour, week, month, year, or even decade of Christ's return. But we are to have a growing sense of urgency that His coming is close—it is within a generation.

There is a major difference in how we live and what we choose to do with our time if we believe something is going to happen within our lifetime, and it may happen at any moment. We live with a much greater concern about how we spend our time and our resources. We do our work, but always with one eye open to the Lord's appearing. We enjoy our lives, but always in anticipation that the Lord may appear at any moment.

There is nothing unfilled in the Scriptures that would preclude the Lord Jesus coming in this generation. Are we alert to that possibility? Are we eagerly anticipating that "today may be the day"?

Third, Jesus said these great words of comfort: "Heaven and earth will pass away, but My words will by no means pass away" (v. 33). All that Jesus has said about His coming *will* occur. We can count on Jesus' words to be true.

- *What additional insights do you have into this passage from Luke?*

  _____

  _____

- *How do you feel about these words of Christ Jesus?*

  _____

  _____

What the Word Says

Watch, stand fast in the faith, be brave, be strong. Let all that you do be done with love. (1 Cor. 16:13–14)

But the end of all things is at hand; therefore be serious and watchful in your prayers. And above all things have fervent love for one another. (1 Peter 4:7–8)

Therefore let us not sleep, as others do, but let us watch and be sober. For those who sleep, sleep at night, and those who get drunk are drunk at night. But let us who are of the day be sober, putting on the breastplate of faith and love, and as a helmet the hope of salvation. For God did not appoint us to wrath, but to obtain salvation through our Lord Jesus Christ, who died for us, that whether we wake or sleep, we should live together with Him. Therefore comfort each other and edify one another, just as you also are doing. (1 Thess. 5:6–11)

What the Word Says to Me

- *What new insights do you have into the coming of Christ and our preparation for that glorious surprise?*

  _____

  _____

- *In what specific ways are you feeling challenged in your spirit?*

  _____

  _____

LESSON 6

THREE PARABLES ABOUT THE LORD'S RETURN

The bulk of Jesus' teaching about His return and the events leading up to it can be found in Matthew 24–25, Mark 13, and Luke 21. I encourage you to read these four chapters in their entirety.

In Matthew 25, we find two parables of Jesus that are well known. They are directly related to the end of the age and Christ's return, and more important, they deal directly with our preparation for Christ's return.

The Parable of the Ten Virgins

As you read through the following parable, take special note of the fact that nobody knew the precise timing of the bridegroom's arrival for his bride. This was customary in Jesus' day. A man and wife were betrothed—legally bound to each other in a ceremony between the two families (at which the bride might not even be in attendance)—but the bride and groom did not live together or have a sexual relationship until the time of their wedding. The wedding might take place as long as a year after the betrothal.

During this period between betrothal and wedding, the bridegroom prepared a home for his bride and set things in order for their life together. The bride prepared herself physically and emotionally for her marriage. The bridegroom might come at any time for his bride—her responsibility was to be ready to go at a moment's notice.

After the bridegroom claimed his bride from her father's house, he escorted her back to their new home—with those in the wedding party lighting the way, singing and dancing joyously in a grand procession through the streets of the village or city. A wedding feast was held, generally lasting a full week, at which time the bride and groom were crowned the "king" and "queen" of their new home and many blessings were voiced. A wedding was one of the most wonderful celebrations in the life of any person or community in Bible times.

Jesus said to His disciples that He was going to "prepare a place" for them and that He would return for them (John 14:2–3). He is clearly the bridegroom in this parable. The bride is the church for whom the bridegroom is coming—the virgins are those who are the attendants of the bride, the ones who accompany the bride and expect to be part of the wedding party for the entire celebration. Jesus said,

> Then the kingdom of heaven shall be likened to ten virgins who took their lamps and went out to meet the bridegroom. Now five of them were wise, and five were foolish. Those who were foolish took their lamps and took no oil with them, but the wise took oil in their vessels with their lamps. But while the bridegroom was delayed, they all slumbered and slept. And at midnight a cry was heard: "Behold, the bridegroom is coming; go out to meet him!" Then all those virgins arose and trimmed their lamps. And the foolish said to the wise, "Give us some of your oil, for our lamps are going out." But the wise answered, saying, "No, lest there should not be enough for us and you; but go rather to those

who sell, and buy for yourselves." And while they went to buy, the bridegroom came, and those who were ready went in with him to the wedding; and the door was shut. Afterward the other virgins came also, saying, "Lord, Lord, open to us!" But he answered and said, "Assuredly, I say to you, I do not know you." Watch therefore, for you know neither the day nor the hour in which the Son of Man is coming. (Matt. 25:1–13)

- *What initial insights do you have into this passage?*

_____

_____

- *How do you feel about the five virgins who had sufficient oil? How do you feel about those who did not have oil?*

_____

_____

I want you to note four things in this parable that relate to our preparation for Christ's return:

First, those in the wedding party "slumbered and slept" because the bridegroom was "delayed." There are many in the church today who have stopped looking for the Lord's return; some don't even believe that He is coming again. They are "asleep" or are "drowsy" when it comes to Christ's coming.

Second, the virgins who did not have sufficient oil in their lamps had plenty of time to purchase oil, trim the wicks of their lamps, and get ready for the bridegroom's coming. They were not unprepared because of a lack of knowledge or a lack of time. They were unprepared because they simply did not do what they knew to do.

Third, the wise virgins did not share their oil because they could not share. None of us can give to another person the Holy Spirit who resides within us.

Fourth, the lack of preparation on the part of the five foolish virgins resulted in their being shut out of the wedding feast. They not only missed the joy of the processional; they missed the celebration. The consequence of their lack of preparation is great.

What does it mean to have sufficient oil in our lamps? Oil throughout the Scriptures is a symbol of the Holy Spirit. The Holy Spirit comes to dwell within us at the time we receive Jesus as our Savior. But it is up to us daily to ask the Holy Spirit to "fill" us. This daily filling of the Holy Spirit means that we totally submit ourselves to the Holy Spirit and seek His guidance, direction, and counsel for all we say and do. We submit our will to His will, saying as Jesus said, "Not my will, but Thine be done." We are willing to follow the leading of the Holy Spirit as we face each decision, confront each problem, or encounter each person who comes across our path.

The Holy Spirit operates in us only according to the degree that we invite Him to do so. It is up to us, as an act of our will, to ask that He fill us daily.

Those who do not have oil in their lamps are those who attend church but who have never confessed their sin to the Lord, believed in the atoning sacrifice of Jesus Christ on the cross, or received God's forgiveness of their sin and the presence of His Spirit within. They have "played" at church but have not been genuinely saved.

This parable stands also as a great warning to those who are lukewarm in their commitment to the Lord, and those who are not actively seeking to follow the Lord.

What the Word Says	What the Word Says to Me
I bow my knees to the Father of our Lord Jesus Christ, from whom the whole family in heaven and earth is named,	_____ _____ _____ _____

that He would grant you,
according to the riches of His
glory, to be strengthened with
might through His Spirit in the
inner man, that Christ may
dwell in your hearts through
faith; that you, being rooted
and grounded in love, may be
able to comprehend with all
the saints what is the width
and length and depth and
height—to know the love of
Christ which passes knowledge; that you may be filled
with all the fullness of God.
(Eph. 3:14–19)

The Parable of the Three Servants

Jesus also told this parable about His return:

The kingdom of heaven is like a man traveling to a far country, who called his own servants and delivered his goods to them. And to one he gave five talents, to another two, and to another one, to each according to his own ability; and immediately he went on a journey. Then he who had received the five talents went and traded with them, and made another five talents. And likewise he who had received two gained two more also. But he who had received one went and dug in the ground, and hid his lord's money. After a long time the lord of those servants came and settled accounts with them. So he who had received five talents came and brought five other talents, saying, "Lord, you delivered to me five talents; look, I have gained five more talents besides them." His lord said to him, "Well done, good and faithful servant; you were faithful over a few things, I will make you ruler over many things. Enter into the joy of your lord." He also who had received two talents came and said, "Lord, you delivered to me two talents; look, I have gained two more talents besides them." His lord said to him, "Well done, good and faithful servant; you have been faithful over a few things, I will make you ruler over many things. Enter into the joy of your lord." Then he who had received the one talent came and said, "Lord, I knew you to be a hard man, reaping where you have not sown, and gathering where you have not scattered seed. And I was afraid, and went and hid your talent in the ground. Look, there you have what is yours."

But his lord answered and said to him, "You wicked and lazy servant, you knew that I reap where I have not sown, and gather where I have not scattered seed. So you ought to have deposited my money with the bankers, and at my coming I would have received back my own with interest. Therefore take the talent from him, and give it to him who has ten talents. For to everyone who has, more will be given, and he will have abundance; but from him who does not have, even what he has will be taken away. And cast the unprofitable servant into the outer darkness. There will be weeping and gnashing of teeth." (Matt. 25:14–30)

- *What initial insights do you have into this passage.*

_____

_____

- *How do you feel as you read this passage? Specifically, how do you feel about the servants who wisely invested their talents? About the one who did not invest his talents wisely? About the "lord" in this parable?*

_____

_____

I would like to call your attention to three specific things in this parable.

First, this parable is about the "kingdom of heaven." It is a spiritual story about a spiritual kingdom. While we may see principles related to the wise use of our material resources and even the wise use of our God-given talents and aptitudes that we have from birth, this story is primarily about spiritual matters.

Second, the one thing that the Lord Jesus gave to those who followed Him as He prepared to go to the Father in heaven was the Holy Spirit. He said, "I will pray the Father, and He will give you another Helper, that He may abide with you forever—the Spirit of truth, whom the world cannot receive, because it neither sees Him nor knows Him; but you know Him, for He dwells with you and will be in you. I will not leave you orphans; I will come to you" (John 14:16–18). Part of the Holy Spirit's function in our lives is to remind us of the words of Jesus and the commandments of Jesus (see John 15:26–27).

When we receive the Holy Spirit into our lives, we automatically receive two things that the Holy Spirit imparts: one or more spiritual gifts (see Rom. 12:4–8), and the "fruit-bearing" nature of the Holy Spirit, which we manifest in our lives the more we abide in the Lord and in His Word (see John 15:5–8; Gal. 5:22–23).

If we apply these principles to the parable of the three servants, we see that these servants, and we as believers in Christ Jesus today, have been given *spiritual* talents. It is the Lord's intent that we *use* them. And as we do, He does a multiplying work in us and through us to others. He takes the use of our spiritual gifts and the fruit of our character to build up the "wealth" of souls and strong believers in His kingdom.

Third, the servant who did not use his spiritual gift, even in the "easiest" way, was severely reprimanded. In sharp contrast, both of the servants who invested their talents experienced a doubling of their talents and they were rewarded with more spiritual gifts and great joy!

The question each of us must ask is this: What am I doing with the spiritual gift(s) imparted to me by the Holy Spirit?"

What the Word Says	**What the Word Says to Me**
[Jesus said immediately before His ascension,] "It is not for you to know times or seasons which the Father has put in His own authority. But you shall receive power when the Holy Spirit has come upon you; and you shall be witnesses to Me in Jerusalem, and in all Judea and Samaria, and to the end of the earth." (Acts 1:7–8)	------------------------------------- ------------------------------------- ------------------------------------- ------------------------------------- ------------------------------------- ------------------------------------- ------------------------------------- ------------------------------------- ------------------------------------- ------------------------------------- -------------------------------------
[Jesus said,] "I am the vine, you are the branches. He who abides in Me, and I in him, bears much fruit; for without Me you can do nothing. If anyone does not abide in Me, he is cast out as a branch and is withered; and they gather them and throw them into the fire, and they are burned. If you abide in Me, and My words abide in you, you will ask what you desire, and it shall be done for you. By this My Father is glorified, that you bear much	------------------------------------- ------------------------------------- ------------------------------------- ------------------------------------- ------------------------------------- ------------------------------------- ------------------------------------- ------------------------------------- ------------------------------------- ------------------------------------- -------------------------------------

fruit; so you will be My disciples. (John 15:5–8)

For as we have many members
in one body, but all the members do not have the same
function, so we, being many,
are one body in Christ, and
individually members of one
another. Having then gifts dif-
fering according to the grace
that is given to us, let us use
them: if prophecy, let us
prophesy in proportion to our
faith; or ministry, let us use it
in our ministering; he who
teaches, in teaching; he who
exhorts, in exhortation; he who
gives, with liberality; he who
leads, with diligence; he who
shows mercy, with cheerful-
ness. (Rom. 12:4–8)

The fruit of the Spirit is love,
joy, peace, longsuffering, kind-
ness, goodness, faithfulness,
gentleness, self-control.
Against such there is no law.
And those who are Christ's
have crucified the flesh with
its passions and desires. If we
live in the Spirit, let us also
walk in the Spirit. (Gal.
5:22–25)

The Parable of the Working and Watching Servants

In Mark 13, we have a third parable that the Lord told about His return:

> Take heed, watch and pray; for you do not know when the time is. It is like a man going to a far country, who left his house and gave authority to his servants, and to each his work, and commanded the doorkeeper to watch. Watch therefore, for you do not know when the master of the house is coming—in the evening, at midnight, at the crowing of the rooster, or in the morning—lest, coming suddenly, he find you sleeping. (vv. 33–36)

- *What initial insights do you have into this parable?*

_____

_____

- *How do you feel as you read this parable?*

_____

_____

- *Have you ever been "caught" not doing what it is that you were expected or assigned to do? What were the consequences?*

_____

_____

Notice that this man gave "authority" and "work" to each of his servants before he went to a far country. Jesus also gave His disciples authority over all manifestations of evil (see Mark 16:16–17) and *work* assignments—specifically the work of being witnesses, winning souls, and preaching and teaching the gospel in all nations (see Matt. 28:18–20).

Also like the master in this parable, Jesus gave an additional command. As His servants, we are not only to do our work with His authority, but we are to watch for His return (Mark 13:37). We are to live in anticipation of His coming.

What the Word Says	**What the Word Says to Me**
And Jesus came and spoke to them, saying, "All authority has been given to Me in heaven and on earth. Go therefore and make disciples of all the nations, baptizing them in the name of the Father and of the Son and of the Holy Spirit, teaching them to observe all things that I have commanded you; and lo, I am with you always, even to the end of the age." (Matt. 28:18–20)	-------------------------------------
[Jesus said,] "Go into all the world and preach the gospel to every creature. He who believes and is baptized will be saved; but he who does not believe will be condemned." (Mark 16:15–16)	-------------------------------------
Then He called His twelve disciples together and gave them power and authority over all demons, and to cure diseases. He sent them to preach the kingdom of God and to heal the sick. (Luke 9:1–2)	-------------------------------------

After these things the Lord appointed seventy others also, and sent them two by two before His face into every city and place where He Himself was about to go. Then He said to them, "The harvest truly is great, but the laborers are few; therefore pray the Lord of the harvest to send out laborers into His harvest . . . Heal the sick there, and say to them, 'The kingdom of God has come near to you.' . . . He who hears you hears Me, he who rejects you rejects Me, and he who rejects Me rejects Him who sent Me." (Luke 10:1–2, 9, 16)

- *What new insights do you have into the ways of our preparation for the Lord's coming?*

- *In what specific ways are you feeling challenged today?*

WHY IS JESUS COMING AGAIN?

Perhaps the central question to the Lord's return is one that very few people ever stop to consider: Why is Jesus coming again? The short and simple answer is this: to finish the work He began the first time He walked this earth. The question then needs to be asked, Why did Jesus come the first time?

It is in knowing why Jesus came the first time that we have our answer as to why Jesus is coming again—His first coming is our backdrop for understanding what it is that He will finish or complete when He comes again.

The Scriptures give us five distinct reasons that Jesus came to the earth as a baby born in Bethlehem, to live and to die, to be raised from the dead, and to ascend back to heaven. Those reasons, in summary, are:

1. To fulfill the law
2. To reveal the Father
3. To testify to the truth
4. To seek and save the lost
5. To reveal life at its best

In this lesson, we will take a brief look at each of these reasons and the way these purposes of Christ Jesus are going to be fulfilled when He comes again. We also see in these five purposes distinct ways in which we are to prepare ourselves for His coming.

To Fulfill the Law

Jesus said of Himself, "Do not think that I came to destroy the Law or the Prophets. I did not come to destroy but to fulfill. For assuredly, I say to you, till heaven and earth pass away, one jot or one tittle will by no means pass from the law till all is fulfilled" (Matt. 5:17–18).

What is the law that Jesus came to fulfill? It was a two-part law—first, the moral law as given to Moses, primarily the Ten Commandments. These laws regarding human behavior in relationship to both God and man were and are God's unchanging standard for regulating the conduct of mankind. This moral law applies to all people, Gentiles and Jews alike. It is a law that is in effect even for nonbelievers, even though they may not acknowledge it and routinely break it.

The second aspect of law that Jesus came to fulfill was the legislative, judicial, and ceremonial system of "religion" that was handed down to Moses. This law pertains to the Jews only and does not apply to Gentiles.

What does it mean for Jesus to "fulfill" the law? Obviously, from what Jesus said in Matthew 5:17, to fulfill is not to replace, put an end to, or dismiss. Jesus lived in obedience to the law. He fulfilled it in these ways: He "lived out" all of the signs and predictions made in the Old Testament about the Messiah and He died as the final definitive atoning sacrifice for sin. In addition, He came to expound upon and explain the full meaning of the moral law. In the Sermon on the Mount (Matt. 5–7) we see a number of instances in which Jesus went beyond the "letter of the law" to explain fully the spirit of the law and the meaning undergirding the law.

Notice that Jesus said He came to fulfill the law and the prophets. In Matthew 22:37–40 Jesus said, "'You shall love the

LORD your God with all your heart, with all your soul, and with all your mind.' This is the first and great commandment. And the second is like it: 'You shall love your neighbor as yourself.' On these two commandments hang all the Law and the Prophets." Jesus came to fulfill the words of the prophets, who repeatedly called the people to obedience to God's commandments and admonished them in the way they were to live. Jesus fulfilled the prophets by showing us how to love God with our whole heart, soul, and mind, and how to love our neighbors as ourselves.

• *What new insights do you have into Matthew 22:37–40?*

_____

_____

Jesus was the Father's final or "full" expression of how a human being is to live. Jesus embodied all of the law in the way He lived His life, and in so doing, He showed us that it is possible to keep the letter of the law only if we first choose to believe and keep the spirit of the law.

• *In your life, have you had experiences in which you kept the "letter" of the law (including God's law) but not the "spirit" of the law? What were the results?*

_____

_____

When Christ comes again, He calls those who have believed in Him to the ultimate expression of a law fulfilled. His law will become the law of the entire world. We will live forever in a state of worship before the Father—serving Him and praising Him with all of our heart, soul, and mind. And we will live in a state of complete harmony and unity with all other believers.

Our challenge as we prepare for the Lord's return is simply this: We are to be worshiping God in the fullness of our own lives, and we are to be expressing love to others at all times.

What the Word Says	**What the Word Says to Me**
I say then: Walk in the Spirit, and you shall not fulfill the lust of the flesh. For the flesh lusts against the Spirit, and the Spirit against the flesh; and these are contrary to one another, so that you do not do the things that you wish. But if you are led by the Spirit, you are not under the law. (Gal. 5:16–18)	....
If you really fulfill the royal law according to the Scripture, "You shall love your neighbor as yourself," you do well. (James 2:8)	....
Bear one another's burdens, and so fulfill the law of Christ. (Gal. 6:2)	....
Rejoice in the Lord always. Again I will say, rejoice! Let your gentleness be known to all men. The Lord is at hand. Be anxious for nothing, but in everything by prayer and supplication, with thanksgiving, let your requests be made known	....

to God; and the peace of God, which surpasses all understanding, will guard your hearts and minds through Christ Jesus. (Phil. 4:4–7)

To Reveal the Father

Jesus said in praying to His Father, "You loved Me before the foundation of the world. O righteous Father! The world has not known You, but I have known You; and these have known that You sent Me. And I have declared to them Your name, and will declare it, that the love with which You loved Me may be in them" (John 17:24–26).

Jesus came to show us the nature of God, and specifically the nature of God as our heavenly Father.

Throughout the generations, God had revealed Himself in a progressive revelation to His people. He gave them various names by which they might "know" Him. In revealing Himself as Elohim, He called them to an understanding of His infinite power and faithfulness. In revealing His name Yahweh, He revealed that He was the eternal One, in personal relationship with His people. He gave His name Adonai to show that He was the Master and Lord of His people.

When Jesus came, He summed up all the names of God previously revealed in one word: *Father*. It is from our loving heavenly Father that all things come. We are to live in relationship to the Father as children to a loving, generous, just, and always-present daddy. We are to know that just as a child bears the likeness of his or her father, so we are to bear the likeness of God our Father in the way we live and treat others.

A person cannot fully know God apart from Jesus. There is no other means for discovering fully the forgiveness of God, the fact that God answers prayer, the way in which God meets needs, or the personal meaning of life. There is no other basis on which to have hope for resurrection and life after death.

When Jesus comes again, He will fulfill His role as *Messiah*, which has also been translated "Delivering Prince." Jesus is the Prince, our Father is the sovereign King—when Jesus returns we will have a full understanding that Jesus is King of kings and Lord of lords. He is the full reflection of the sovereign One, bearing all of the authority and power of a king. Furthermore, we who believe in Him will rule and reign with Him.

How are we to prepare for the coming of our "daddy" King? By preparing ourselves as His children, His princes and princesses. We are to seek to become like Christ in every way, doing all that we can to grow into the fullness of Christ's character.

What the Word Says

Jesus said to him, "Have I been with you so long, and yet you have not known Me, Philip? He who has seen Me has seen the Father." (John 14:9)

He is the image of the invisible God, the firstborn over all creation. (Col. 1:15)

For in Him dwells all the fullness of the Godhead bodily. (Col. 2:9)

For it pleased the Father that in Him all the fullness should dwell, and by Him to reconcile all things to Himself. (Col. 1:19–20)

What the Word Says to Me

To Testify to the Truth

Pilate asked Jesus, "Are You a king then?" Jesus answered, "You say rightly that I am a king. For this cause I was born, and for this cause I have come into the world, that I should bear witness to the truth. Everyone who is of the truth hears My voice" (John 18:37).

What is the truth to which Jesus testifies? On what truth is our King's kingdom established? Perhaps the most succinct statement of His truth is found in John 3:

> Most assuredly, I say to you, unless one is born of water and the Spirit, he cannot enter the kingdom of God. That which is born of the flesh is flesh, and that which is born of the Spirit is spirit. Do not marvel that I said to you, "You must be born again." The wind blows where it wishes, and you hear the sound of it, but cannot tell where it comes from and where it goes. So is everyone who is born of the Spirit . . . No one has ascended to heaven but He who came down from heaven, that is, the Son of Man who is in heaven . . . For God so loved the world that He gave His only begotten Son, that whoever believes in Him should not perish but have everlasting life. For God did not send His Son into the world to condemn the world, but that the world through Him might be saved. He who believes in Him is not condemned; but he who does not believe is condemned already, because he has not believed in the name of the only begotten Son of God . . . Everyone practicing evil hates the light and does not come to the light, lest his deeds should be exposed. But he who does the truth comes to the light, that his deeds may be clearly seen, that they have been done in God. (3, 5–8, 13, 16–18, 20–21)

- *What new insights do you have into this passage?*

_____

_____

• *Have you ever had an experience in which you tried to cover up the truth (or the truth of something you did)? What were the results? What did it mean to you to be "set free" to tell the truth?*

The truth that Jesus came to proclaim can perhaps be summed up in one sentence: God desires that man be set free from the bondage of sin and guilt and be fully reconciled in love to God and to one another. Jesus is the full embodiment of that truth (see John 14:6).

When Jesus comes again, He comes to set us free from all temptation to sin. When we are with Him, we will be totally beyond the bounds of evil influence; we will be freed from a world that still groans under the weight of sin. We will be in the loving presence of God the Father without any inhibiting influence by our fleshly nature.

How are we, then, to prepare for the Lord's return? We are to seek God's righteousness in all that we say, do, think, and believe. We are to pursue the truth at all times, and become quick to discern deceit and lies in all their many forms.

What the Word Says

[Jesus said,] "I am the way, the truth, and the life. No one comes to the Father except through Me." (John 14:6)

[Jesus said,] "The Spirit of the LORD is upon Me,
Because He has anointed Me
To preach the gospel to the poor;

What the Word Says to Me

He has sent Me to heal the
brokenhearted,
To proclaim liberty to the cap-
tives
And recovery of sight to the
blind,
To set at liberty those who are
oppressed;
To proclaim the acceptable
year of the LORD." (Luke
4:18–19; see Isa. 61:1–2)

[Jesus said,] "And you shall
know the truth, and the truth
shall make you free." (John
8:32)

To Seek and Save the Lost

Jesus said, "The Son of Man has come to seek and to save
that which was lost" (Luke 19:10).

In Jesus' great parable of the loving father (also called the
parable of the prodigal son), Jesus paints this picture of God
the Father: "When he [the prodigal son] was still a great way
off, his father saw him and had compassion, and ran and fell
on his neck and kissed him" (Luke 15:20). What a wonderful
picture this is of our loving heavenly Father! He is forever seeking our return to Him. He is continually seeking our salvation
from our old selves.

The result of seeking is finding. Jesus said, "Seek, and you
will find" (Matt. 7:7). When Jesus comes again, we will be fully
found and saved from all sin forever. We, in turn, will "fully
find" our Lord—we will know Him in dimensions we cannot
even imagine now. We will also know ourselves and others as
God knows us (see 1 Cor. 13:12).

As we await the Lord's return, we must continually seek to

know the Lord more intimately. We must seek to understand ourselves so that we can release old hurts and wounds to the Lord and be healed of them. We must desire spiritual growth—continually working out our salvation in practical ways so that we might become increasingly whole as human beings, spirit, mind, and body.

What the Word Says	What the Word Says to Me
For now we see in a mirror, dimly, but then face to face. Now I know in part, but then I shall know just as I also am known. (1 Cor. 13:12)	
Therefore, if anyone is in Christ, he is a new creation; old things have passed away; behold, all things have become new. Now all things are of God, who has reconciled us to Himself through Jesus Christ, and has given us the ministry of reconciliation, that is, that God was in Christ reconciling the world to Himself, not imputing their trespasses to them, and has committed to us the word of reconciliation . . . For He made Him who knew no sin to be sin for us, that we might become the righteousness of God in Him. (2 Cor. 5:17–19, 21)	

To Reveal Life at Its Best

Jesus said, "I have come that they may have life, and that they may have it more abundantly" (John 10:10). Jesus came to reveal to us by the example of His own life two things: the fact that we can have an abundant life, and how to live an abundant life.

A life in Christ is marked by those things we call the fruit of the Holy Spirit: love, joy, peace. It is a life marked by freedom from guilt and sin, a life of reconciliation to others as manifested in forgiveness, patience, goodness, faithfulness, gentleness. It is a life marked by self-control and victory over the lust of the flesh, the lust of the eyes, and the pride of life. It is the life that every person longs to live. (See Gal. 5:22–23.)

When Jesus comes again, He adds the crowning facet to the abundant life—perfection for all eternity. He takes abundance to the nth degree—bringing us to a fullness of love, joy, and peace. He provides that perfection to the nth degree of time and space: eternity.

We are to prepare for His coming by seeking to walk by the Spirit and in the Spirit. We are to bear increasingly the fruit of the Spirit in our lives. To walk in the Spirit is to know the abundant life of Christ and to know a life beyond compare.

What the Word Says	What the Word Says to Me
Now to Him who is able to do exceedingly abundantly above all that we ask or think, according to the power that works in us, to Him be glory in the church by Christ Jesus to all generations, forever and ever. (Eph. 3:20–21)	....

For you were once darkness, but now you are light in the Lord. Walk as children of light (for the fruit of the Spirit is in all goodness, righteousness, and truth), finding out what is acceptable to the Lord. (Eph. 5:8–10)

Surely goodness and mercy shall follow me
All the days of my life;
And I will dwell in the house of the LORD
Forever. (Ps. 23:6)

- *What new insights do you have into the reason for Christ's return?*

- *What new insights do you have into the way in which you are to prepare for His return?*

- *In what specific ways are you feeling challenged in your spirit?*

THE RAPTURE OF THE CHURCH

One of the great hopes and joys of those who may be alive when the Lord returns is a biblical event called the "Rapture." As we mentioned earlier in this book, the word *Rapture* is not in the Bible. Through the generations, this event has come to be called the Rapture, and it is also called the "snatching away" or the "taking away" of the church.

We read about the Rapture in 1 Thessalonians 4:15–18:

> For this we say to you by the word of the Lord, that we who are alive and remain until the coming of the Lord will by no means precede those who are asleep. For the Lord Himself will descend from heaven with a shout, with the voice of an archangel, and with the trumpet of God. And the dead in Christ will rise first. Then we who are alive and remain shall be caught up together with them in the clouds to meet the Lord in the air. And thus we shall always be with the Lord. Therefore comfort one another with these words.

- *What initial insights do you have into this passage?*

_____

_____

- *What are your feelings as you read this passage?*

_____

_____

I want to call your attention to four aspects of this passage in Thessalonians:

First, the Lord is the One who is calling His people. Those who are unsaved are not able to hear the voice of the Lord (see John 10:4–5). The Rapture is only for believers.

Second, the Lord calls from heaven and we respond instantly to His call. In Revelation 4:1 we read, "After these things I looked, and behold, a door standing open in heaven. And the first voice which I heard was like a trumpet speaking with me." The Lord's voice is a heralding, trumpetlike call to us—a signal to which we hearken and respond. In the Greek language in which this passage was first written, the word *shout* is a word used to refer to a military officer barking a command. The trumpet is a call used to "herald the assembling of a group of people." When we hear the Lord calling to us, we will have no hesitation in our obedience.

Third, the Lord's call will be a summons to *all* believers, both those alive at that time and those who have died. A woman once said to me about a summer camp experience she had: "They had a bell that they would ring. It was a signal that we were all to gather together immediately in the central courtyard. It didn't matter if you were in a cabin or in the dining hall or playing softball or swimming in the pool. When the bell rang, you quit what you were doing and immediately went to the courtyard. There were some parents at the camp who had gone to the same camp when they were children—and when the bell sounded, even these parents left what they were doing and went to the courtyard." That's the way the Lord's summons will be for us. The dead who are with the Lord and about His business in heaven will come immediately. We who are alive and on earth will come immediately. We will all be gathered together as one body.

Fourth, we will never be separated from the Lord again. The Rapture is not a brief, "rapturous" experience in which we feel caught up in the Holy Spirit. It is a permanent shifting of our existence. We will be forever with the Lord from that moment on.

What the Word Says	What the Word Says to Me
[Jesus said,] "You do not believe, because you are not of My sheep, as I said to you. My sheep hear My voice, and I know them, and they follow Me. And I give them eternal life, and they shall never perish; neither shall anyone snatch them out of My hand. My Father, who has given them to Me, is greater than all; and no one is able to snatch them out of My Father's hand. I and My Father are one." (John 10:26–30)	_____

An Immediate Change

The Rapture will illicit an immediate response from us and result in an immediate change in us. Paul wrote to the Corinthians:

We shall not all sleep, but we shall all be changed—in a moment, in the twinkling of an eye, at the last trumpet. For the trumpet will sound, and the dead will be raised incorruptible, and we shall be changed. For this corruptible must put on incorruption, and this mortal must put on immortality. So when this corruptible has put on incorruption, and this mortal has put on immortality, then shall be brought to pass the saying that is written: "Death is swallowed up in victory." (1 Corinthians 15:51–54)

- *What new insights do you have into this passage?*

_____

_____

- *What is your emotional response to this passage from Corinthians?*

_____

_____

In Bible times, the twinkling in a person's eye was considered to be the briefest unit of time possible. Quickly here, quickly gone. That is the nature of the Rapture. In a moment so brief and instantaneous we cannot measure it, we will be raised and changed.

What is the change we will experience? We will receive glorified bodies. The bodies we currently know as our "flesh" will be instantly changed into a physical form that is recognizable but does not decay or bear any ability to experience sickness, pain, or limitation. It is because our bodies are changed instantly that we are able to respond instantly to the Lord's call.

Our physical removal. The Rapture results in our physical removal from this earth. As Jesus said, "Two men will be in the field: one will be taken and the other left. Two women will be grinding at the mill: one will be taken and the other left" (Matt. 24:40–41). Not only will we be changed in the Rapture, but the nature of the whole earth will be changed. It will be as if all "leaven" has been removed from humanity. Those who embody the Holy Spirit will be removed from the earth.

- *How do you feel as you read Matthew 24:40–41?*

_____

_____

A Judgment for Christians

The change that we experience in the moment of the Rapture will be a change that includes an instant judgment of us who are believers. We cannot enter fully into the presence of the Lord and remain there forever without this judgment.

The judgment that Christians face is not a judgment related to sin, but rather, to our works as believers. To be in the presence of the Lord is to "see" instantly the full scope of our works as the Lord sees them.

Read how John describes the appearance of the Lord: "I heard behind me a loud voice, as of a trumpet . . . Then I turned to see the voice that spoke with me. And having turned I saw seven golden lampstands, and in the midst of the seven lampstands One like the Son of Man, clothed with a garment down to the feet and girded about the chest with a golden band. His head and His hair were white like wool, as white as snow, and His eyes like a flame of fire" (Rev. 1:10, 12–14).

When the Lord looks at us with His eyes of fire—eyes of pure holiness searing into the depths of our being—truly we will be known fully by Him and we will fully know ourselves. We will see all that we didn't do, could have done, could have had, could have been. All that wasn't and isn't will be burned up by His holiness and what remains will be of Him—it will be eternal, it will be pure, and it will be rewarded. The more that remains, the greater the reward. Paul also wrote of this to the Corinthians:

> According to the grace of God which was given to me, as a wise master builder I have laid the foundation, and another builds on it. But let each one take heed how he

builds on it. For no other foundation can anyone lay than that which is laid, which is Jesus Christ. Now if anyone builds on this foundation with gold, silver, precious stones, wood, hay, straw, each one's work will become clear; for the Day will declare it, because it will be revealed by fire; and the fire will test each one's work, of what sort it is. If anyone's work which he has built on it endures, he will receive a reward. If anyone's work is burned, he will suffer loss; but he himself will be saved, yet so as through fire. (1 Cor. 3:10–15)

• *What insights do you have into this passage?*

_____

_____

The purpose of our judgment as believers according to our works is so that anything that is not of the Lord may be burned away from us forever and we, therefore, might be completely pure as we enter into His eternal presence. This final refinement of our souls as we enter into a state in which we are never separated from the Lord produces in us the very glory of the Lord. It creates holiness and wholeness in us, so that we are completely without fault or blame, sin or any desire to sin. What a great and glorious day that will be for us!

What the Word Says

Blessed be the God and Father of our Lord Jesus Christ, who has blessed us with every spiritual blessing in the heavenly places in Christ, just as He chose us in Him before the foundation of the world, that we should be holy and without blame before Him in love, hav-

What the Word Says to Me

_____

_____

_____

_____

_____

_____

_____

_____

_____

ing predestined us to adoption as sons by Jesus Christ to Himself, according to the good pleasure of His will, to the praise of the glory of His grace, by which He made us accepted in the Beloved. In Him we have redemption through His blood, the forgiveness of sins, according to the riches of His grace which He made to abound toward us in all wisdom and prudence . . . that in the dispensation of the fullness of the times He might gather together in one all things in Christ, both which are in heaven and which are on earth—in Him. (Eph. 1:3–8, 10)

Who can stand when He appears?
For He is like a refiner's fire
And like launderers' soap.
He will sit as a refiner and a purifier of silver;
He will purify the sons of Levi,
And purge them as gold and silver,
That they may offer to the LORD
An offering in righteousness. (Mal. 3:2–3)

Beware of Mockers

Peter warned that the Rapture is such a mysterious and awesome event that there will be those who scoff at the very idea, saying that it isn't rational or scientific. He wrote,

> Beloved, I now write to you this second epistle . . . that you may be mindful of the words which were spoken before by the holy prophets, and of the commandment of us, the apostles of the Lord and Savior, knowing this first: that scoffers will come in the last days, walking according to their own lusts, and saying, "Where is the promise of His coming? For since the fathers fell asleep, all things continue as they were from the beginning of creation." (2 Peter 3:1–4)

- *In your experience, have you encountered those who discount the Lord's return or mock the very idea of the Rapture? Have you yourself had this feeling?*

_____

_____

Peter went on to write this about the reason for the seeming delay of the Lord's coming:

> But, beloved, do not forget this one thing, that with the Lord one day is as a thousand years, and a thousand years as one day. The Lord is not slack concerning His promise, as some count slackness, but is longsuffering toward us, not willing that any should perish but that all should come to repentance. (2 Peter 3:8–9)

The Lord is going to call for His people. He will bring us into His presence, a purified people to live with Him forever. And the Rapture will be instantaneous. There will be no oppor-

tunity for any response to the Rapture other than to partici-
pate in it fully if we are a believer in Christ Jesus, or to be left
out of it completely if we are not.

- *What new insights do you have into our preparation for the
  Lord's call to us?*

  _____

  _____

- *In what ways are you feeling challenged in your spirit today?*

  _____

  _____

THE RAPTURE AND OTHER END-TIME EVENTS

A discussion about the Rapture of the church generally evokes two questions:

1. When does the Rapture occur with regard to the Great Tribulation?

2. Is the Rapture the same thing as the second coming of Christ?

We will deal specifically with these two questions in this lesson.

At the outset, let me point out to you that the Bible has more than twenty times the verses about the Day of the Lord and the second coming of Christ than it does about the "first coming" of Jesus. A great deal has been written about the Great Tribulation and the Second Coming (Day of the Lord) in both the Old Testament and New Testament. Our purpose here is not to give a comprehensive account of end-time events, but rather, to point out the distinctions among events and our need for preparation now so that we will not experience God's wrath.

The Rapture and the Great Tribulation

A period of great tribulation is described in the Scriptures. This is not "normal" tribulation—which is a general term for trouble, trial, or sorrow—as described by Jesus when He said, "In the world you will have tribulation; but be of good cheer, I have overcome the world" (John 16:33). The Great Tribulation is a seven-year period of great terrifying trouble on the earth.

This period is first described by the prophet Daniel, and it is also described in vivid detail by John in the book of Revelation.

The wrath of God. During the Great Tribulation, the wrath of God is poured out. The Great Tribulation is a time of judgment. God has three main purposes for this period.

First, the Lord will use the suffering of the Great Tribulation to call 144,000 people from Israel to be His witnesses on the earth to prepare for the Messiah's appearance.

Second, the Lord will send witnesses to preach the gospel to the remaining Gentiles on the earth.

Third, Satan will be given full opportunity to do his work through the Antichrist (also called the Beast) and the False Prophet, after which time Satan will be bound.

What is the timing of the Rapture with regard to the Great Tribulation? Opinions have been divided through the years. Some believe the Rapture occurs before the Tribulation and sets the starting point for the Tribulation; some believe the Rapture occurs midway in the Tribulation (at a period of three and one half years); and some believe that the Rapture occurs immediately before the end of the Tribulation and the second coming of Christ. I believe that the Rapture occurs before the Great Tribulation for these two primary reasons:

First, we are told repeatedly in the Scriptures to be "ready" for an unannounced, unpredictable Rapture that could occur at any moment. If the Rapture does not occur until after events of the Great Tribulation begin, the imminence and surprise element of the Rapture are negated.

Second, we are never told in Scripture that Christians will experience the wrath of God that is designated for nonbelievers. The Great Tribulation is a time of tremendous woes that encompass the entire earth. Furthermore, there is no mention of the church in the various manifestations of God's wrath described in Revelation from chapters four onward.

There are those who believe that Christians will somehow be "cleansed of sin" and "made more holy" by the events of the Great Tribulation. Throughout the New Testament, there is no means by which a person is cleansed from sin *other than* the shed blood of Jesus. Suffering does not cleanse us—our acceptance of Jesus' death on our behalf and the forgiveness offered by God the Father through our belief in Jesus bring us to the point where the Holy Spirit cleanses us. Events and circumstances do not cleanse or make us holy—only God does that divine spiritual work in our lives.

Finally, there would be little reason for Paul to tell the church repeatedly to "comfort one another" with the truth of the Rapture if the church was going to experience the Great Tribulation. There will be little reason for hope or comfort during those frightful, terrible years.

As you read through the verses below about the Great Tribulation (as well as the surrounding verses), you will find no mention of believers experiencing God's wrath and there is no word of advice as to how believers might endure these events.

Record not only your insights about these verses, but also your emotions.

What the Word Says	What the Word Says to Me
Seventy weeks are determined For your people and for your holy city, To finish the transgression, To make an end of sins,	....

To make reconciliation for
iniquity,
To bring in everlasting
righteousness,
To seal up vision and
prophecy,
And to anoint the Most Holy.
(Dan. 9:24)

Then I saw another sign in
heaven, great and marvelous:
seven angels having the seven
last plagues, for in them the
wrath of God is complete.
(Rev. 15:1)

Then I heard a loud voice
from the temple saying to the
seven angels, "Go and pour
out the bowls of the wrath of
God on the earth." (Rev. 16:1)

And there shall be a time of
trouble,
Such as never was since there
was a nation,
Even to that time.
And at that time your people
shall be delivered,
Every one who is found written in the book.
And many of those who sleep
in the dust of the earth shall
awake,
Some to everlasting life,

Some to shame and everlasting
contempt.
Those who are wise shall shine
Like the brightness of the fir-
mament,
And those who turn many to
righteousness
Like the stars forever and ever.
(Dan. 12:1–3)

The Rapture and the Second Coming

The Second Coming of Christ is also called the Day of the Lord in the Scriptures. This is a time when those remaining on the earth during the Great Tribulation and those who have died without accepting Jesus as their Savior are judged. The Rapture and the Second Coming differ in these distinct ways:

- The Rapture is for all believers; the Second Coming involves the "elect" who have "endured" to the end of the Great Tribulation (1 Thess. 4:16–17; Matt. 24:31).
- The Rapture results in believers joining together with the Lord "in the air"; at the Second Coming, the Lord comes to earth to set up His earthly reign (1 Thess. 4:17; Matt. 25:31–34).
- At the Second Coming, the nations of the earth are judged and the sheep are separated from the goats (Matt. 25:31–33; Zech. 14).
- The Rapture is imminent—it could happen at any time; the Second Coming follows a series of predicted events (Matt. 24).
- There is no mention of Satan at the Rapture; at the time of the Second Coming, Satan is bound (Rev. 20:1).
- The Rapture is sudden, without warning, and is experienced in its fullness only by believers; at the Second Coming, every eye will see the Lord (Rev. 1:7).

- The Rapture is an event that is to bring hope and comfort to the heart of the believer; the Second Coming is a time when the tribes of the earth will mourn (Rev. 1:7).

As you read through the verses below about the Second Coming, record both your feelings and your insights.

What the Word Says	What the Word Says to Me
Behold, He is coming with clouds, and every eye will see Him, even they who pierced Him. And all the tribes of the earth will mourn because of Him. (Rev. 1:7)	----------------------------------- ----------------------------------- ----------------------------------- ----------------------------------- ----------------------------------- -----------------------------------
After these things I heard a loud voice of a great multitude in heaven, saying, "Alleluia! Salvation and glory and honor and power belong to the Lord our God! For true and righteous are His judgments, because He has judged the great harlot who corrupted the earth with her fornication; and He has avenged on her the blood of His servants shed by her." (Rev. 19:1–2)	----------------------------------- ----------------------------------- ----------------------------------- ----------------------------------- ----------------------------------- ----------------------------------- ----------------------------------- ----------------------------------- ----------------------------------- ----------------------------------- -----------------------------------
[Jesus said,] "And there will be signs in the sun, in the moon, and in the stars; and on the earth distress of nations, with perplexity, the sea and the waves roaring; men's hearts	----------------------------------- ----------------------------------- ----------------------------------- ----------------------------------- -----------------------------------

failing them from fear and the expectation of those things which are coming on the earth, for the powers of the heavens will be shaken. Then they will see the Son of Man coming in a cloud with power and great glory." (Luke 21:25–27)

[Jesus said,] "When the Son of Man comes in His glory, and all the holy angels with Him, then He will sit on the throne of His glory. All the nations will be gathered before Him, and He will separate them one from another, as a shepherd divides his sheep from the goats. And He will set the sheep on His right hand, but the goats on the left." (Matt. 25:31–33)

Then the LORD will go forth
And fight against those nations,
As He fights in the day of battle.
And in that day His feet will stand on the Mount of Olives,
Which faces Jerusalem on the east . . .
Thus the LORD my God will come,
And all the saints with You . . .

And the LORD shall be King
over all the earth.
In that day it shall be—
"The LORD is one,"
And His name one. (Zech.
14:3–5, 9)

Multitudes, multitudes in the
valley of decision!
For the day of the LORD is
near in the valley of decision.
The sun and moon will grow
dark,
And the stars will diminish
their brightness.
The LORD also will roar from
Zion,
And utter His voice from
Jerusalem;
The heavens and earth will
shake. (Joel 3:14–16)

Fire and devastation. The Day of the Lord is repeatedly associated with fire and devastation. The prophet Joel wrote:

> A fire devours before them,
> And behind them a flame burns;
> The land is like the Garden of Eden before them,
> And behind them a desolate wilderness;
> Surely nothing shall escape them. (Joel 2:3)

The prophet Zephaniah gives this word of the Lord:

> "I will utterly consume everything
> From the face of the land,"
> Says the LORD;

"I will consume man and beast;
I will consume the birds of the heavens,
The fish of the sea,
And the stumbling blocks along with the wicked.
I will cut off man from the face of the land,"
Says the LORD. (Zeph. 1:2–3)

- *What insights do you have from these passages about the Day of the Lord?*

_____

_____

This complete renovation of the earth establishes the "environment" in which the Lord will work to create a "new heaven and a new earth" for His millennial reign.

And What of Christ's Own During These Events?

What will those who have loved and served the Lord Jesus Christ be doing during these days of great tribulation and at the time of the judgment of the Second Coming?

The Scriptures hold out the promise that we will be in praise before the throne of God. We will be crying,

You are worthy, O Lord,
To receive glory and honor and power;
For You created all things,
And by Your will they exist and were created. (Rev. 4:11)

We will be saying with a loud voice:

Worthy is the Lamb who was slain
To receive power and riches and wisdom,
And strength and honor and glory and blessing! . . .

Blessing and honor and glory and power
Be to Him who sits on the throne,
And to the Lamb, forever and ever!" (Rev. 5:12–13)

How then can we prepare for these days? By increasing our praise and worship! Praise is one thing that we can do on this earth that we will continue to do through all eternity. Read what the psalmist foretells as the role of the saints in judging the nations with the Lord Jesus Christ:

Let the saints be joyful in glory;
Let them sing aloud on their beds.
Let the high praises of God be in their mouth,
And a two-edged sword in their hand,
To execute vengeance on the nations,
And punishments on the peoples;
To bind their kings with chains,
And their nobles with fetters of iron;
To execute on them the written judgment—
This honor have all His saints.
Praise the LORD! (Ps. 149:5–9)

- *What new insights do you have into the return of the Lord and our preparation for His return?*

  _____

  _____

- *In what specific ways are you feeling challenged in your spirit?*

  _____

  _____

LESSON 10

THE THREE W'S

Repeatedly in these lessons and throughout the Scriptures we find three admonitions given to us about the Lord's return:

1. Watch faithfully
2. Work diligently
3. Wait peacefully

We Are to Watch

The Lord said repeatedly that we are to watch for His coming because we do not know the day or hour of Christ's appearing (Matt. 24:42; 25:13; Mark 13:35). Jesus gave this specific instruction in Luke 21:36, "Watch therefore, and pray always that you may be counted worthy to escape all these things that will come to pass, and to stand before the Son of Man."

Prayer is not the only thing we are to be doing as we watch. We are to stand fast in the faith, with courage and strength (see 1 Cor. 16:13). We are to watch soberly, arming ourselves with faith and love and salvation (see 1 Thess. 5:8). As we watch, we are to be especially aware of false prophets; we are to discern the spirits and to reject soundly all who do not confess that Jesus Christ has come in the flesh and is God (see 1 John 4:1–2; 2 Peter 2:1).

Jesus spoke to John in a vision and gave this great promise to those who are watchful: "Behold, I am coming as a thief.

Blessed is he who watches, and keeps his garments, lest he walk naked and they see his shame" (Rev. 16:15).

- *In your experience, what is the most difficult part about watching for something that doesn't appear immediately?*

_____

_____

What the Word Says	What the Word Says to Me
[Jesus said,] "Watch and pray, lest you enter into temptation. The spirit indeed is willing, but the flesh is weak." (Matt. 26:41)	---------------------------------- ---------------------------------- ---------------------------------- ---------------------------------- ----------------------------------
Watch, stand fast in the faith, be brave, be strong. Let all that you do be done with love. (1 Cor. 16:13–14)	---------------------------------- ---------------------------------- ---------------------------------- ----------------------------------
But the end of all things is at hand; therefore be serious and watchful in your prayers. And above all things have fervent love for one another. (1 Peter 4:7–8)	---------------------------------- ---------------------------------- ---------------------------------- ---------------------------------- ---------------------------------- ----------------------------------
But let us who are of the day be sober, putting on the breastplate of faith and love, and as a helmet the hope of salvation. For God did not appoint us to wrath, but to obtain salvation through our Lord Jesus Christ, who died	---------------------------------- ---------------------------------- ---------------------------------- ---------------------------------- ---------------------------------- ---------------------------------- ----------------------------------

for us, that whether we wake
or sleep, we should live
together with Him. (1 Thess.
5:8–10)

We Are to Work

Why does Jesus leave us here on the earth after we are saved? Why is it that we aren't born again and immediately die? Because we still have work to do! That work is twofold: evangelism and conformation. These two areas of work are not sequential; rather they are to be simultaneous.

Evangelism

Our first work is one of winning souls. We are to be the Lord's witnesses—telling of the love of God and the atoning death of Jesus Christ for sin. We are to testify about what the Lord has done in our own lives, both with our words and by the example of our lives. As long as there is a soul on earth who hasn't heard the gospel of our Lord Jesus Christ, we have work to do!

What the Word Says	**What the Word Says to Me**
The fruit of the righteous is a tree of life, And he who wins souls is wise. (Prov. 11:30)	
But sanctify the Lord God in your hearts, and always be ready to give a defense to everyone who asks you a reason for the hope that is in you, with meekness and fear. (1 Peter 3:15)	

Conformation to Christ

Our second area for work is within our own selves—we are to seek to grow spiritually into an ever-increasing intimacy with the Lord. None of us is fully living up to our spiritual potential. We all have room to grow. And the more we look at the life of Jesus Christ and experience His love . . . and the more we seek to walk daily by the leading of the Holy Spirit who indwells us . . . the more we see ourselves in relationship to the Lord, and the more we see in our own lives that is unlike Him. It is in those areas where we discover we are not like Christ that we must seek to be conformed to His likeness. Our minds must be renewed (see Rom. 12:1). Our inner hurts and emotions must be healed. We must grow in our spiritual discernment and in the wisdom of God. Our faith must be strengthened and used so that our prayers and our actions are effective in building up the Lord's kingdom.

As we are conformed to the likeness of Christ and brought to maturity in Christ, we will find ourselves being used increasingly to edify or to build up others. Our conformation as individuals is part of the greater conformation of the entire church to be the living, active body of Christ on the earth. (See the IN-TOUCH Bible study *Pursuing a Deeper Faith.*)

What the Word Says	What the Word Says to Me
I beseech you therefore, brethren, by the mercies of God, that you present your bodies a living sacrifice, holy, acceptable to God, which is your reasonable service. And do not be conformed to this world, but be transformed by the renewing of your mind, that you may prove what is	-------------------------------

that good and acceptable and perfect will of God. (Rom. 12:1–2)

For whom He foreknew, He also predestined to be conformed to the image of His Son, that He might be the firstborn among many brethren. (Rom. 8:29)

Beloved, now we are children of God; and it has not yet been revealed what we shall be, but we know that when He is revealed, we shall be like Him, for we shall see Him as He is. And everyone who has this hope in Him purifies himself, just as He is pure. (1 John 3:2–3)

For the grace of God that brings salvation has appeared to all men, teaching us that, denying ungodliness and worldly lusts, we should live soberly, righteously, and godly in the present age, looking for the blessed hope and glorious appearing of our great God and Savior Jesus Christ, who gave Himself for us, that He might redeem us from every lawless deed and purify for

Himself His own special people, zealous for good works.
(Titus 2:11–14)

We Are to Wait in Peace

Waiting isn't easy for many people. Impatience is often manifested by frustration. Waiting can also cause a buildup of fear
in some people—the longer something anticipated doesn't happen, the greater the concern with what will happen, which can
degenerate into what might happen. Once we begin to imagine
what might happen, fear is only a step away.

The angels spoke peace to the earth at Jesus' first coming
(see Luke 2:14). More than four hundred times in the
Scriptures, the Lord says that we are not to fear, but rather,
we are to have peace. The prophet Isaiah referred to Jesus as
the Prince of Peace (Isa. 9:6). Throughout His ministry, the
Lord Jesus spoke peace—to a woman with an issue of blood
He said, "Go in peace"; to a stormy sea He said, "Peace be
still"; and to His disciples He said, "My peace I give you." The
Lord calls us to peace as we await His return.

Apart from Jesus, there is no peace—not within a human
heart, and not among human beings or nations. With Jesus, we
can experience peace that passes our rational minds and settles
deep within (Phil. 4:7). It is peace that we are to seek and
peace that we are to find as we await the Lord's return.

What the Word Says	What the Word Says to Me
[Jesus said,] "Peace I leave with you, My peace I give to you; not as the world gives do I give to you. Let not your heart be troubled, neither let it be afraid." (John 14:27)	---------------------------- ---------------------------- ---------------------------- ---------------------------- ---------------------------- ----------------------------

[Jesus said,] "These things I have spoken to you, that in Me you may have peace." (John 16:33)

Comfort each other and edify one another, just as you also are doing. (1 Thess. 5:11)

Be anxious for nothing, but in everything by prayer and supplication, with thanksgiving, let your requests be made known to God; and the peace of God, which surpasses all understanding, will guard your hearts and minds through Christ Jesus. (Phil. 4:6–7)

- *What new insights do you have into our preparation for the Lord's return?*

- *In what specific ways are you feeling challenged in your spirit?*

CONCLUSION

WHAT IS YOUR ANSWER?

When the Lord comes, will He find you among those who love Him and call Him Savior and Lord?

When the Lord comes, will He find you doing what He has commanded you to do?

When the Lord comes, will He find you eager to see Him?

When the Lord comes, will He find you "ready" for His appearing?

When the Lord calls with a shout from heaven, will you instantly rise to be with Him?

When the Lord appears in the clouds, will your heart rejoice with exceedingly great joy?

You have it within your will to answer these questions. How will you choose to respond to the Lord's challenges upon your life?

The fact is . . . He is coming again!